MALLED

OTHER TITLES BY KIT DOBSON

Please, No More Poetry: The Poetry of derek beaulieu (editor)

Producing Canadian Literature: Authors Speak on the Literary Market-place (with Smaro Kamboureli)

Transnational Canadas: Globalization and Anglo-Canadian Literature

Transnationalism, Activism, Art (co-editor with Áine McGlynn)

MALLED

DECIPHERING SHOPPING IN CANADA

KIT DOBSON

WOLSAK
& WYNN

Cover image: dubes sonego / Shutterstock.com
Cover and interior design: Marijke Friesen
Author's photograph: Aubrey Jean Hanson
Typeset in Dante
Printed by Ball Media, Brantford, Canada

The image on p. 78 is from *Scott Pilgrim & The Infinite Sadness*, by Bryan Lee O'Malley, Oni Press, Portland, OR, 2006, reprinted with permission of the publisher.

Poems from *Mannequin Rising*, by Roy Miki, New Star Books, Vancouver, BC, 2011, reprinted with permission of the author and publisher.

Poems from *The Word for Sand*, by Heather Spears, Wolsak and Wynn Publishers, Toronto, ON, 1988, reprinted with permission of the publisher.

The publisher gratefully acknowledges the support of the Canada Council for the Arts, the Ontario Arts Council and the Government of Canada.

Wolsak and Wynn Publishers, Ltd.
280 James Street North
Hamilton, ON
Canada L8R 2L3

Library and Archives Canada Cataloguing in Publication

Dobson, Kit, 1979–, author
    Malled: deciphering shopping in Canada / Kit Dobson.

ISBN 978-1-928088-46-2 (softcover)

1. Consumption (Economics)–Social aspects–Canada.
2. Shopping malls–Canada. 3. Shopping malls–Social aspects–
Canada. 4. Shopping centers–Canada. 5. Shopping centers–Social
aspects–Canada. 6. Shopping–Social aspects–Canada. I. Title.

HC79.C6D627 2017   306.30971   C2017-904876-7

This one is for Aubrey Jean Hanson.

CONTENTS

Preface

It is the summer of 2017 as this book heads toward publication. A lot has happened during the course of writing this book – the travels that have led to it span more than five years – and a lot more will happen. By the middle of 2017, it is clear that the landscape of shopping is changing anew. Alongside it, so too will the cultures of shopping take new directions.

In North America, 2017 is being written up as a year of mass store closures, especially in the United States.[1] That country is in a state of uprising while I write these words, with the old wounds of a racist history resurfacing in the present. On the economic front, from major department stores like Macy's to retailers like Crocs, every week seems to yield another announcement of more boarded up shopfronts. In Calgary, where I am writing this preface, downtown commercial vacancies are hovering at around twenty-five per cent.[2] It is unclear how we will look back on this time of market uncertainty, layoffs, industrial change, NAFTA renegotiations and CEOs abandoning US President Donald Trump. From inside the moment, however, it looks as though this time might herald a genuine series of changes.

Changes, however, are seldom straightforward. In the case of the cultures of shopping, the changes look perhaps more circular than anything. Earlier this spring, I found myself fortunate enough to be travelling, this time to Poland. Poland is a country from whence some of my forebears came to Canada, and I had always been keen to travel there. I was grateful for the opportunity. In the cities of both Kraków and Katowice, I couldn't help but notice the large, new malls, the Galeria Krakowska and the Galeria Katowicka. Both were built this millennium and both connect directly to their respective city's train stations. They are large, modern, efficient and sleek, with broad glassworks making the most of the available natural light. Both were busy, bustling, active.

What was remarkable about these two malls? They were, on the one hand, very similar to North American malls, at least on the surface, though these ones were particularly tidy and new feeling. Many of the stores were the same as ones back home, which still feels remarkable to me in a country that was, way back in my childhood, "behind the Iron Curtain," as the adults would have said.

More remarkable, though, was the way in which these malls showed how shopping changes in unpredictable ways. I don't think that either of these malls is a direct imitation of North American style, in spite of my first reactions. That analysis would be too easy to make at a time when conventional indoor malls in North America are closing up fast.

Instead, as I walked around the malls, in one city and then the other, I was struck once again at how shopping develops cultures of its own. That novelists, poets, graphic writers, visual artists and filmmakers choose to use malls and other spaces of consumption in their work just makes sense. What remains interesting, to me, is how infrequently we take notice. Instead, consumerism and shopping fade into the background, wallpapering our days but rarely taking centre stage. But the cultures are there.

PREFACE

In "If These Malls Could Talk," writer and performer Vivek Shraya writes of Edmontonians' love-hate relationship with shopping malls. The piece accompanied the 2015 release of the multi-authored zine *The Magnificent Malls of Edmonton*, which Shraya edited. In the piece, Shraya suggests that Edmonton's malls are, in spite of their faults, "magnificent." They are magnificent "because, despite how we begrudge them or dismiss them, they hold our quiet, unassuming, everyday, ordinary memories – the ones we almost forgot. We grow up in, around and through these malls and don't even notice."[3] A zine like Shraya's, however, brings the malls back into focus, forces us to notice how they are there, how they are parts of our memories and of our cultural lives, too.

As the times change yet again, as they always do, malls will change too. Shopping shifts. The death of the mall, which I note in this book has been proclaimed many times, is, in the end, not the real story. It seems to me that the story, instead, is one about how and where we come together. It is a story about where we congregate, where we build communities, where we laugh and cry. Shopping is a complicated thing, but in order to live, human animals (and other animals too) need to consume air, water and food, at a minimum, in order to persist on this sometimes-too-cold, sometimes-too-hot rock. Very quickly we discover that we are consumers, and very quickly that consumption can be enlisted as part of a capitalist culture that moulds our consumption in particular ways. What shape that consumption takes – and what shape it will take – says a lot about who we are and who we will be.

In the Beginning: Shoes

My lifetime favourite shoes were the blue Grover shoes, Buster Brown brand, that I owned when I was about six years old. They were totally awesome Sesame Street cross-marketed shoes, blue canvas with Velcro straps. I wore them everywhere I went and enjoyed the fact that I could do them up with little effort.

Those shoes, however, met their match on one trip to my grandparents' farm in northern Alberta. My grandparents on both sides once had small family farms on either side of the town of Athabasca, an hour and a half north of Edmonton, near the divide between Treaty 6 and Treaty 8 territories. The town sits on the banks of the troubled Athabasca River, but significantly upstream from the bitumen extraction projects associated with Fort McMurray and places farther to the north. By the time that I came along, only the farm on my father's side, to the south of town, was still in the family. I loved visiting the farm and spent time there in every season. I remember it in crisp, vivid detail, from northern lights to summer solstice. On that fateful late-summer trip, I was there with my parents and my sister, hanging out and enjoying life. The farm was always a busy, bustling place, and I would join my Granny on walks to feed the chickens and sheep, or to tour the pastures and see the cattle and check the fences for any fallen trees pressing down on the barbed wire. A dog or two accompanied us, and my Granny taught me to recognize plants and shared a thing or two about life. I would sometimes ride the tractor with my grandfather, too, as he fed the cows or ploughed the fields.

One day during that trip, out in the cow paddock, I stepped in a deep, fresh cow patty. I remember the squelching feeling of pulling my feet out from the ankle-deep muck. It turned out that cow shit does not come off of canvas any too easily. Try as we might, the shoes just wouldn't come clean. They looked, instead, a new shade of grey-brown. I was crushed.

That event, however, wasn't enough to deter me from my love of my lovable furry blue monster shoes. I kept them on while I was out building a tree house with my dad in the days that followed. I walked everywhere in them, right up until I walked along – balancing, my arms out and my eyes watching the spot where the poplars and birch trees met the sky – an old board that we were reusing to build the tree house. The board, unfortunately, had old nails sticking out of it. I stepped on one and it went right through the worn sole of my Grover shoe and maybe an inch or so into the sole of my foot. I remember my father picking me up and carrying me into the farmhouse to wash and bandage my foot. So long, shoes.

Although it was some thirty-plus years ago now, the thing that I remember with the most precision from that time was those shoes. My mother would likely say that I'm exaggerating points of the story, and she may well be right. I could still draw an accurate map of the farm, right down to where the gooseberries were, or drive there without thinking about it, but it's the shoes that stand out. A lot of time has passed since then, and, as it's done so, I've thought more and more about what it means to be so attached to those physical objects that surround us. Why do we care so much about our shoes? And yet, when I ask people, it seems like, on the balance, they do; most people can name a favourite pair without much hesitation. We are attached, stitched into, the cultures of shopping from early on in our lives.

Introduction: Chinook Centre

I started this book because I hated the mall. Today is December 26th, 2014. I am in Calgary's Chinook Centre – at the mall – so that I can enjoy the spectacle that takes place on this day, as it has on every Boxing Day throughout my life. In recent years, Chinook Centre has been able to count on over one hundred thousand shoppers to visit the mall each year on Boxing Day, making it a great day for sales, as well as a great day to liquidate merchandise that hasn't moved well all year. (I check afterward, when typing up these words from my old-fashioned pen-and-paper notebook: one source says that one hundred and eight thousand shoppers came on Boxing Day 2014, or close to one-tenth of Calgary's population.[1]) The markdowns today get people shopping, and the credit card debt ratchets up a notch for all.

I have been coming to Chinook Centre on Boxing Day for the past few years (2012 excepted, as you'll see in the conclusion of this book). I often come with my partner or sometimes with my sister, when she is in town, but no one else was ready to tolerate the lines or the busyness of the general mayhem this year, so I've come on my own. I've been doing my best to make a sport out of it, to have fun with it. I think of my malling on Boxing Day not as a serious attempt to shop, but rather as a chance to participate in a display of human behaviour that would look as strange to any visiting alien species as it must to the birds.

I arrived about an hour before I started writing. I began with an end-to-end walk-through in order to get my bearings. Chinook Centre is a mall that runs north-south; its main pedestrian corridor branches in a few places toward exits or smaller wings. Aside from the parkades and the office tower, it is two storeys tall. The open galleries in many of the corridors allow you to look from one floor to the other. The mall has been redone in beige tile work – off-white, really – with white walls, wood accents and subtle skylights that supplement the halogen and fluorescent lighting throughout. The exits, as is conventional in postmodern mall architecture, are out of the way. You don't see them while shopping unless you are looking for them. Demographically, this mall caters to an aspiring, young, middle-class crowd. People seem to dress up to come to Chinook. I have at least managed to put on pants. From where I am sitting, I can see several security cameras pointed at me and my fellow shoppers. The stores are what we might think of as "everyday posh": Nordstrom, Anthropologie, Scotch & Soda and the Apple Store are all within a few strides of me. I could spend a few thousand dollars (that I don't have) with the swipe of a card, thanks to the rather reckless system of credit that we have evolved in North America.

My first walk-through has suggested to me that today is going to be busy, but that it could be less busy than it has been the last few years. Or at least that's how it feels. Last year, there was a cordon to limit how many people could get into Victoria's Secret at a time; the same was true for Banana Republic. I don't see any red velvet ropes this year. I wonder if the Black Friday phenomenon is picking up as much steam in Canada as it seems to be and, as a result, is taking some of the punch away from December

26th. I still think of Black Friday first and foremost as Buy Nothing Day, the annual challenge to avoid consumerism launched by Vancouver's *Adbusters* magazine. Today, however, consumerism appears to be winning out. Boxing Day has long been the biggest shopping day of the year, but the US tradition of having massive sales linked to their Thanksgiving weekend has spilled north of the 49th parallel. But Black Friday doesn't seem to be as big a deal here – at least not yet. Or, at least, no one died while shopping in Canada this year on Black Friday, so the event doesn't seem as threatening. Sadly, dying while Black Friday shopping is a common enough occurrence that there is a macabre website, blackfridaydeathcount.com, devoted to cataloguing such events.

I ran into one of my students during my walk-through – he works as a plainclothes security guard at a women's clothing store. I typically run into one or two people I know whenever I visit Chinook. It is the closest indoor shopping mall of any size near to where I live – and Calgary's oldest example of an enclosed mall – and it is also the closest one to the home I lived in as a teenager.

After I finish my walk-through, I return to the entrance where I started and get myself a tea in a wax paper cup. I need to pace myself today. I sit at a large table in the middle of the corridor. The wide table seats eight, and I am at one corner. People come and go as I sit here and write. At first, a young woman wearing a deliberately tacky Christmas sweater sits at the other extreme corner of the table. Next comes a middle-aged South Asian couple who sit opposite me, then a pair of white teenage girls beside me, and then two Asian women at the other end of the table. No one sits for long. The food kiosks in this spot are for simple recharges, not substantial meals. This is a spot for caffeine and carbohydrates mostly – as I've been having too (with a good-sized tea spill on my notebook to show for it). In the time that I sit here, hundreds of people file by, each bag that they hold proof of having conquered another long line. By and large, their purchases are smaller in size than I might have expected.

A security guard strolls by, and I wonder if my presence here, writing in the mall, will draw any attention. The people who notice me either glance right over or else stare quizzically, and briefly. I am interested in how strangers interact with each other. One of our ongoing family projects is something that we call Sushi Quest, a perpetual search for Calgary's best sushi. Our best results tend to be unexpected ones, little hole-in-the-wall places in suburban strip malls, run by families. We have a set of rules for Sushi Quest, one of which is that, if given the option, we always sit as close to the window as possible, so that we can get a good view and see what happens. Doing so inevitably seems to bring more people in the door. People like to be around other people, but, at the same time, they'd rather not be too close, either. The people at my table are replaced by a young, very blond family. The two boys, who are about five or six, look at me, look at my journal. Their mother very pointedly does not look at me.

Best shopping slogans of the day so far: "shop. schlep. repeat." (on a cloth carrier bag) and "get it or regret it" (on a store wall). The moral imperative to shop remains strong years after George W. Bush made the outlandish claim that shopping was one way to defeat terrorism. I finish my tea and get up, ready for a move.

—

I never expected to move back to Calgary.

When I was eighteen, I couldn't leave fast enough. I grew up in cities around Canada, but ended up in Calgary for those formative teenage years – the ones that many of us might want to leave behind afterward. Among the things that prompted me to leave was the city's culture of rapacious consumerism, a culture that was symbolized, for me, by the malls. I was complicit in this culture, but I wanted to shift it into my past. When I was in high school, I spent a lot of time in malls (all of which look different today): in Chinook Centre, that ever-growing space of upwardly mobile middle-class consumption; in the northwest's Market Mall, a slightly more modest and practical alternative close to the University of Calgary; at Southcentre, then a slightly rundown mall at what was at the time the southern end of the city, which offered some different storefronts; and in the +15 maze downtown – the above-ground skyway – where shopping connects to office towers and apartment blocks (a place that I return to in the conclusion of this book). I also sought the used bookshops and cafés of the northwest's Kensington neighbourhood, and the strip of oddities along 17th Avenue and 4th Street in the city's southwest. Other places existed, like the more working-class and racialized malls of the north- and southeast, and the hodgepodge of Inglewood, but my zone was mainly the southwest.

Why was I there, in the mall, so much? In the 2006 Gary Burns and Jim Brown film *Radiant City*, a film made in Calgary, we see the sprawling suburbs of the city coming into being. Although the city is never named in the film, Calgary is one of the targets of this satirical mockumentary. We see characters snarled in the traffic on Deerfoot Trail, isolated in their bizarre tract homes cut out of the prairie topsoil, trying to deal with disjointed lives on faceless streets and, importantly, going shopping. What appears at first to be a documentary turns out to be a false one, and we see that the focal family in the film is, in fact, a series of non-professional actors – people who live lives analogous to those portrayed in the film. I've often wondered how those actors feel about their lives in the aftermath of participating in a satire of themselves. One of the things that remains clear in the film is that Calgary risks being a caricature of itself, or rather that its stereotypes (oil and gas, cowboy cultures, SUVs and endless suburbia) risk coming closer to the truth than Calgarians might like to admit, even though the city is always changing and has, in my view, changed very much and for the better. One of my favourite statistics about Calgary is that it occupies a slightly larger geographical footprint than all of New York City, but has only a little bit more than an eighth of the population.[2] And yet, some small signs of densification strategies are starting to pop up; maybe that, too, will change.

It's in cities like Calgary that malls have proliferated. The last generation's champion of urban spaces, Jane Jacobs, hated malls. To her, they signalled precisely what is wrong with post–Second World War urban environments. She argued that malls work because they hold a monopoly on commercial spaces.[3] In suburbs, residential streets lead to strip malls; the streets on which strip malls are situated lead to larger malls; there are no integrated commercial or office spaces. You have to drive from your residence in order to get anywhere besides other residences, the net effect of which is the destruction of complete neighbourhood communities.

When I walk or drive through the lesser thoroughfares of Calgary, I often find myself wondering why they aren't designed with commercial storefronts along the streets, with affordable apartments above (as you might find in cities like, say, Toronto, Montreal, New York, London or elsewhere). The answer, in part, is the mall: there is no need for commercial spaces within neighbourhoods because everything is in the mall, and in larger quantities too. Local shops would, and do, fail. As a result, communities stutter and fail in turn, and the city is evermore clogged with traffic that goes nowhere – and then the city builds more roads in order to compensate. Which of course has the effect of creating more traffic by making it possible to build more suburban tract housing. And so on. Jane Jacobs' thinking, on this issue at least, has long struck me as being spot on; she was a canny observer of human behaviour.

As I was saying, I left Calgary at eighteen in pursuit of greener pastures. Over the next twelve years, I lived in cities across Canada and in the UK, and travelled and studied and worked at several universities. The mall never went away, but the fabric of the cities I travelled to or lived in showed me different ways of approaching the mall, or approaching the ways in which we consume, and of thinking about how these spaces are thought about culturally. In the meantime, I aged and learned a few things along the way, about politics, life and how to continue to grow, live, love and learn. In the car-friendly (or pedestrian-unfriendly, depending on how you think about it) cities in the west of North America, people drive to shop. In some cities, like many of those on the Prairies, that can account for a lot of how people spend their time. In denser cities like Toronto, Vancouver or Montreal, neighbourhood shops might constitute a greater part of the urban fabric, and making larger purchases is less convenient. In small towns and rural communities, the box store (especially Walmart) seems to have played a role in gutting the old Mom-and-Pop shops on main street. Even while local townships decry the loss – and more people are forced to drive longer distances in order to buy, at best, marginally cheaper goods – this shift continues. I'm not romantic or nostalgic for any form of consumption, not really, not when I think about it academically, but I've found, in the course of my travels and in the course of writing this book, that I am supportive of the small, community-driven store. I want to think through these different ways of getting stuff (often stuff that we don't need) and see the differences that local geographies make in the process.

—

Later on Boxing Day, I wind up in the Chinook Centre food court. Odd name that – it is not particularly courtly. I prefer my partner's use of the term food fair, which at least suggests some of the merry crowdedness and disorder that characterize this milling, slurping, spilling, chomping throng. There is something carnivalesque to the food fair, after all. I opt for mall sushi, which seems like a lesser evil, though I have my doubts about the farmed salmon and plastic packaging. Not a real contender for Sushi Quest. When I was younger, before white people like me had discovered their love of sushi, the food court was in a different part of this mall. That food court was relatively austere, unadorned even, sparsely decorated in pastels and browns. It was next to the old cinema, which had only a couple of screens. I think that I watched one of the Indiana Jones films there when it was first released.

The food court now is a wide-open, three-tiered, bustling affair on the second floor. It has many tables, as well as a carousel, and a handful of inexplicable flying machines circulating on tracks far above our heads. After waiting around for a while, two young men finish their burgers and beckon me to take over their table. From where I sit down, I can see downstairs to the escalator. It's been temporarily shut down and security guards show up at either end. A line of perhaps a hundred people quickly forms. The escalator resumes a few minutes later, but there is now a perpetual backlog of people looking to come upstairs for a bite to eat.

All around me, the tables are full. People are wandering around, looking for tables, texting their friends, clutching their bags. In front of me, the merry-go-round pacifies children. To my right is the escalator and a large sculpture of a Tyrannosaurus rex made of disused machinery. To my left, past the tables, I can look out of a huge bank of windows to see the afternoon sunlight stretching out. The traffic on MacLeod Trail is severely congested by shoppers hoping to find a spot in one of the mall's parking lots. I am glad that I came here with a car from the car-sharing service of which I am a member. With a bit of luck, I will find a similar car in order to get home, or else I will take transit; Chinook is very near to one of the city's light rail transit stations. Parking on Boxing Day is sheer mayhem.

From where I am sitting, I can also see innumerable logos, in all directions, from storefronts to banner ads to food and clothing labels to the bags that people are carrying, right down to the logos on my own shoes. So far, I have only added one bag to my load, from Eddie Bauer. That store may not be the most fashionable, perhaps, or the top ethical choice (from a menu of ethically iffy choices), but their jeans fit me well. I rarely buy new clothing. Much of what I have owned, until recently, has come from thrift shops. Two of my former favourite shirts, which invariably fetched compliments at work, were, embarrassingly enough, salvaged from a free store at a dump. Those shirts, alas, wore out. While I may like nice shoes and so on, I haven't usually been a big spender, for a bunch of predictable reasons: I don't need stuff, I oppose sweatshop labour, I'm cheap and I've spent perhaps too much of my life being insufferably moralistic about many things. But I'm working on all of these concerns in one way or another – learning to be gentler to myself and others – in part by writing this book and figuring out which values are the ones that I hold most dear.

Boxing Day has become one of the few days per year when I will buy myself new stuff. Well, new jeans anyhow. I tend to wear out a pair or two per year. Last year on Boxing Day, I bought myself my first ever pair of swimming goggles. It had, in all serious- ness, never occurred to me before that I could actually own my own goggles. As someone who is highly myopic (sometimes both literally and metaphorically), not having goggles had long fed into my phobia of swimming. Having had weak, infection-prone ears as a child didn't help either, and neither did the time that I nearly drowned in a lake in Ontario. Getting my own goggles allowed me, now in my mid-thirties, to reclaim my ability to swim – and, on sale on Boxing Day, they only cost me eight bucks. I still can't believe that it had never occurred to me to buy my own up until that moment. Unfortunately, they broke, and so I need to replace them.

As I finish eating, the line for the escalator lets up. All around me, people are on the lookout for tables. As much as I'm enjoying myself, I am waiting for The Despair to set in. The Despair is a familiar feeling I get when I am out shopping, a sort of ennui that reminds me of the awfulness of consumption and that points, in turn, to the existential knowledge of my own mortality (though I do eschew actual despair as a mode of being). I felt it for a mo- ment earlier while riding the escalator at the other end of the mall, but I am, so far, enjoying the mad folly of being a part of this spectacle. I suspect that, at some level, everyone here knows that Boxing Day is a silly excuse for shopping, but that they nev- ertheless play gamely along. That ability to do something that is silly, but to do it in all seriousness, is really one of my favourite things about being human.

As I look toward the escalator again, I see Mark Messier's face on a banner telling me to get a mobile phone and to watch more hockey. After a while, I can't take his grin anymore. It's time to move. Someone will want my table.

———

I moved back to Calgary when I was thirty. The move back was unexpected. I was hired to a good job at a time when I was desperate for stable employment (as too many people of my generation are), and so I jumped at the opportunity. I've returned as a different person, for sure. Now that I am in my mid- (okay, late) thirties, I am less sure of myself – I have less of that youthful hubris, I'd like to think – and I have been through challenging times. I've made decisions that I wouldn't make again and from which I hope I have learned; I've also made a whole heck of a lot of decisions of which I'm very proud. I came to my political consciousness in the context of the counter-globalization and identity politics movements of the 1990s and 2000s, reading Naomi Klein, bell hooks, Judith Butler, Noam Chomsky and Michel Foucault. I have spent a lot of time in activist circles, though I've always been suspicious of calling myself an activist, as the label has never held too much meaning for me – one can be a right-wing activist just as much as a left-wing one, for instance. I think that pursuing a better world is about much more than labels, which can be used to exclude as much as they can be used to include (perhaps even more so). I've done a lot of community organizing around labour, in particular, and in opposition to war. These days, my partner and I have two fantastic daughters, a mortgage, a rundown car that we've managed to pay off, and the daily challenges of trying to raise a family to the best of our abilities, while also contributing as well as possible to our communities. In other words, we are trying to exist with humility and gratitude, living lives that are full of very fertile messiness, trying to avoid fucking too many things up, and coping with plenty of the contemporary pressures with which you, dear reader, are likely only too familiar.

When I am in the mall, I feel sometimes like I've dropped from outer space into a strange land. Then again, I'm also just a dorky middle-aged dude who still wants to be fashionable but is, at the same time, too old to hang with the mallrats (thank goodness, really; no one wants that). I'm cheap, especially when it comes to myself, but I also believe in finding the joy in the world and celebrating every moment that we can.[4] I've lived in many cities in Canada – from west to east, I've lived in Victoria, Vancouver, Calgary, Toronto, Montreal and Halifax – and visited many more, so I have a pretty good context for understanding at least some aspects of this strange federation of provinces and territories.

How, though, to come back to Calgary? I love many aspects of this city, particularly its understated forms of weirdness, but at the same time I really struggle with other aspects of it. When we moved back here, I realized that I would need to make some formal gesture in order to find my peace with the malls that I had blithely left behind at eighteen. This book is that gesture. I have been an inveterate mall-hater, but these things are everywhere. Although perhaps in decline in many places, they are not going away anytime soon. Newer, bigger, fancier malls are being built all the time. Heck, while I'm writing this book the American Dream mall being built in New Jersey is slated to have North America's first indoor ski hill in it. Malls, in other words, persist and continue to mutate. So: I have set out to try to understand what it is about malls like Chinook Centre that might compel ten per cent of a city's population to visit it on Boxing Day every year.

Understanding the mall might seem to some a self-explanatory thing. We go there, we shop, we go home. (Maybe we ski, too.)

We can condemn the mall as being a synecdoche – a stand-in – for everything that is bad about Western society, starting with consumption: we know that we are consuming ourselves to a long, slow death (quicker for some) wrought by environmental destruction. I've read that it would take four Earths to match human consumption if everyone consumed like Albertans do.[5] So the mall is evil and stands for everything that is bad about our world right now. But that fast condemnation is easy – too easy, I think. There is a lot more to it than that in my view. Canadians' relationship to mall spaces might share something with the slacker culture of Kevin Smith's film *Mallrats*, but I think that there's more to the mall than it being a place where the disaffected go to seek belonging of the sort that Brodie, Jason Lee's character, claims in the film. A big part of his motivation in the film is to reclaim a space that he is concerned about losing to the jerks that have taken over, symbolized by Shannon, played by Ben Affleck.[6] People go to malls for lots of reasons. Some even go there to shop. Many might say that malls work in Canada because of the weather – it came up often in my conversations. Many seniors and young parents go there in order to walk in the wintertime, thereby avoiding icy sidewalks. Many might say that they are convenient (although Jane Jacobs would tell us otherwise). Many might go there in order to meet people. Many might go because of the entertainment and other amenities on hand. Many might go there, well, because mall.

So. In order to understand how malls and other spaces of consumption work in Canada, I am tracking a few different things at the same time. First of all, I have visited every single shopping space that I discuss in this book (the ones in Canada, anyhow, and some in the US and Europe; I am yet to travel to the new malls of Asia). Many of these travels are ones that I've done over the course of my life, but a lot of my recent travel has been specifically mall-themed. I haven't been able to get to the Avalon Mall in St. John's, or to the Northern Store, but I did what I could. I'm well versed in my mall-hating ways in Calgary and have sought to take that love-hate to new places. One time at Southcentre I did a thorough check in all of the stores after discovering that one store sold what they called a "reader's chair": there wasn't a single store in the mall at that time that sold a book so that you could use the chair according to its appointed purpose. I like books and I don't like malls, see, and I think that balance of likes and dislikes is, by and large, pretty fair. Malls, at least until recently, gave me headaches and often left me despairing at the state of humankind – The Despair is a common result of a shopping trip. And yet, I've been to West Ed aplenty, and ditto the Eaton Centre (in multiple cities, no less). I've gone shopping in Kitsilano and at the problematically named Mic Mac Mall in Dartmouth, Nova Scotia. I know how to shop. I've also gone to many new malls in order to write this book. I've visited malls in ways that I never have before, notebook in hand, and I've been to some places that I'd only ever read about before, too. I've headed to the revamped Montreal Forum, which is now a space of consumption, and I've broken my lifelong boycott of Walmart, all in the name of trying to figure out these strange places.

The second part of this project is to investigate how malls and shopping spaces appear in the culture that gets created in Canada. From Michael Snow's well-known Canada geese, installed in downtown Toronto's Eaton Centre, to the lesser-known art installations in malls across the country, the spaces in which we shop are suffused with culture. Malls also appear – although these appearances are rare enough to be a bit of a surprise – in films, poems, stories and songs. My feeling is that they don't appear as often as they might because malls aren't supposed to be cultural spaces, at least in our everyday imaginary. Are you more likely to write a poem about the grand vista that you find at the summit of a mountain, or about shopping for the boots that take you there? In practice, we may spend more time shopping for our lives outdoors than we do in the outdoors itself (assuming that time outdoors is a part of our practice and demographic). But it's the time outdoors that counts. Similarly, artists appear to be reticent about actually showing the act of consumption itself in many of their works. But not always: malls, shopping and consumption do show up, and I will trace as much of that cultural stuff as I am able to here.

Third, I think that it's important that we understand malls in a variety of ways because there are so many tensions, small and large, that are uncovered when we look closely. While malls are structured so as to seem outside of time, and typically do not have clocks in them – more on that later – they do have a history (just as capitalism in general wants to deny that history exists, all in the name of perpetual growth and renewal, but it never can). Malls haven't always existed, nor will they always exist in the future. Competition from the box store phenomenon and from online shopping, let alone the aerial drones that might, one day soon, deliver our purchases to our doors, show that shopping is changing. There are plenty of articles hailing the death of the mall.[7] Mall architecture changes over time too, even within the relatively brief period during which department stores and then malls have flourished in Canada – a phenomenon discussed in part in Donica Belisle's intelligent book *Retail Nation*.[8]

Malls also have grown to target different demographics with more and more sophistication. Retail spaces cultivate particular audiences, and usually, ideally, the ones that will generate the highest return on investment. In some places, this might mean that malls or individual stores are gendered or racialized or classed according to norms that bear paying close attention to. What that means is that malls and stores target specific people according to expected norms of purchasing behaviour. How actual humans respond to those structures is fascinating in practice, and usually more complex than anticipated, but more and more tracking technologies are being invented all of the time in order to make stores better at targeting their customers. So much remains contested: malls exist in tension with the environments in which they are placed, and this tension is not just that of the immediate neighbourhood, or the friction between sellers and buyers. There is also, for instance, an environmental tension between malls, consumerism and the climate catastrophes that we see unfolding around us every day. All of these tensions, then, are part of my exploration.

Fourth and finally, this exploration is intended as an act of humility and, hopefully, compassion on my part. As I began to write this book, I recognized how I have in the past sounded like (and worse yet, perhaps at times been) an aloof, academic critic of everything. No one likes a person who can only see the negative side of everything, yet my job has trained me to focus specifically on the act of critique. Some academics, who also are tired of being perpetually grim, are thinking about things like affirmative critique. Too often, my profession invites me to meet my peers, my colleagues and the world around me in a spirit of judgment instead of the spirit of forgiveness, kindness and understanding that, more and more, I am working to inhabit in the remainder of my life. In writing this book, then, I am also trying to teach myself about how to appreciate the transitory nature of the mall, how to find and welcome its moments of unexpected beauty. Doing so pushes me to rethink some of my own assumptions about what it means to be a critic. It is too easy, and too haughty, frankly, to accuse everyone who shops in malls of doing so because of their false consciousness: the situation is more complex than that.[9] So I don't, for instance, have too much patience for the sort of denunciations that a writer like Douglas Rushkoff inserts into his book *Coercion*: "Disorientation keeps customers inside the mall. Many malls utilize hexagonal floor plans, which have been proven to be among the most difficult to navigate. Once inside such a mall, the patron must traverse a complicated set of hallways arranged at intentionally confusing angles.... Every turn disorients him further, until he no longer knows in which direction the exit is to be found."[10] While at times I may share that feeling, the underlying thesis here – that shoppers are all dupes – is, I think, far too simple. Instead of relying upon the false consciousness thesis in order to explain shopping, as I think Rushkoff does here, I want to develop a conversation with you that inquires honestly and openly into the act of shopping as a very human sort of thing in which I sometimes participate. If I can become less of a humbug in the process and better recognize the ways in which I, too, am part of this system, then not only might I better be able to think of genuine alternatives, but so too might I become better at connecting with you, because, almost certainly, you shop too.

———

After discovering that Chinook Centre has only two main washrooms, I nip into the cinema at the south end of the mall in order to make use of theirs. I'm sure that some of my more shopping-savvy friends know where all of the secret bathrooms are in this mall, but, sadly, I do not. On the way out, I notice a small section of tables tucked away behind the concession stand. The tables are full and the area is bustling. I ask to share a table with two middle-aged women who are reading on Kobo e-readers. It seems to me like an odd place to read, but then again it's also an odd place to write.

The cinema concourse is loud, ill lit in multiple neon colours and has top-forty music playing. The floors are sticky. It is everything that you would expect from a movie theatre. There is skee-ball and air hockey in one corner. When this cinema was opened, a giant sphinx above the box office would periodically shoot flames from its mouth (at least that's how I remember it). Now, the theatre is decorated in an odd mismatch of faux-Egyptian and contemporary pop themes. You used to buy tickets from plastic statues of Osiris; the card reader and PIN pad were set about where Osiris' genitalia otherwise would have been. Now the ticket dispensers are the same as the ones at cinemas elsewhere.

One thing that this theatre speaks to, and very much so, is contemporary Western society's remarkable ability to absorb a wide range of cultures. There is little intrinsic reason why a cinema that mostly plays standard, English language Hollywood fare should have oversized scarab beetles scuttling up its exterior. But, on the other hand, there is no reason why it shouldn't, either. The culture on display at the mall is a magnificently syncretic one – one that readily absorbs whatever is recognized, is recognizable and that sells. I think of how the English language so readily absorbs words from other languages, giving it the largest lexicon of any planetary language today (though Shakespeare still sounds better in the original Klingon).

A group of teenaged women pass behind me, singing along to the song coming over the speakers. At the next table, a child burps loudly.

That syncretic culture is also, at the same time, one that misses out on a lot of nuance as it colonizes other cultures at will. Hence, in this case, Egypt = Sphinx + Osiris + scarab beetles. The cinema needn't contemplate the complexities of, say, Tahrir Square, the Suez Canal or global geopolitics. In fact, to expect such depth would be absurd and incomprehensible, basically unthinkable in this context. Or, similarly, the music and video store that I visited downstairs, before I came up here, always feels like its selection is shrinking. For instance: I was looking in the punk section for any bands not fronted by men. I couldn't find any obvious examples (though my knowledge of punk may well have failed me – punk itself is a very lively and complex scene). This absence of depth, or reduction effect, was also active in the record store, except there the effect was to reduce punk to music by angry men. Sure, there was music with strong political content that I do like (Propagandhi, for example), but the gender equation and expectations seemed pretty clear as far as that store was concerned. I am far from the first to notice that the culture of capitalism is about the reduction of choice as much as it is about programming choice according to predetermined outcomes. (Apple or Windows? Maybe Linux. Would you like that shirt in red, green or blue?) Seeing the reduction effect at work, however, and recognizing it as such is still jarring. Egypt and punk are both far more complex than what we see on display in the mall. Where can we go if we don't want to participate? Are there ways to participate differently, or does that path just lead to shopping at expensive boutiques, or online at Etsy and the like? In other words, can opting out mean something other than even more individualism? Is there a way to opt differently?

—

In order to follow through on the different questions and threads of this project, the chapters of this book are organized in several ways. First, each chapter focuses on one or several geographically distinct shopping spaces: CrossIron Mills, just north of Calgary; Eaton Centre and Honest Ed's in Toronto; the Montreal Forum and Boulevard St-Laurent; the Walmart in Whitehorse; Kitsilano, Granville Island and the Vancouver suburbs; West Edmonton Mall (of course); and the +15 system in downtown Calgary. There are many cameo appearances as well, by places like Richmond, BC; strip malls on the Prairies; the PATH system in Toronto; the Underground City (RÉSO) in Montreal; and many others.

Each chapter then uses texts, art and films in order to think through the book's main themes: environmentalism and the outdoors; the (im)possibility of escaping from consumer culture; the manufacturing of nostalgia and memory through consumerism; how gender, race and identities structure shopping; the destruction of communities; historical development and growth; and the future. The materials that I look at range widely: from poetry to novels, and from sculptures to films like *Fubar 2*. It turns out that malls do show up in the culture produced in this cold climate quite a bit – but only once you start to look for them.

Most of the time, though, malls remain more or less invisible to our daily cultural lives. I'd like to make us all a little bit more aware of how much time we spend consuming, of how much we use shops and malls – no matter how we might feel about them – and of how ever-present they are in the margins of our imaginaries. Words like "Kevlar," "Teflon" and "Slurpee," the words of everyday life, don't show up very often in poetry written in Canada.[11] We can and should wonder why there are so many poems about trees and lakes when we in fact spend so much of our time in urban concrete jungles. When I started looking, however, I found that shopping and malls do show up. They are in the culture; we just need to take note of the fact.

On that note, a point about the title of the book, *Malled: Deciphering Shopping in Canada*. The working title to the book was a pluralization of a song title from the 1990s, "Mall Culture Superstar," from the Ottawa alterna-punk band Furnaceface. Even though it no longer fit the eventual form that this book took, I'd like to acknowledge, too, how song lyrics have influenced this project. The Furnaceface song is a satirical take on the culture produced by malls; the chorus includes the line "I wanna be whoever you are," and the singer becomes that anonymous face through consumerism, through being a "mall culture superstar." Arriving when the track did – it was officially released on the album *This Will Make You Happy* in 1994 – it was a serious attempt to take the piss out of the commercialization of grunge, which was well underway by then, with shops like the Gap doing a great job of selling the plaid flannel shirts that folks my age had embraced via the Seattle scene. Kurt Cobain was dead by the end of that year, and grunge floundered and then died a commercially induced death. As I began to write this book, that track popped back into my head. I still have that Furnaceface CD, which I borrowed from a girlfriend in high school. I'd be happy to return it (we could exchange: I think that she still has my copy of Hole's *Live Through This*), but it's come in handy while writing so I'm also happy to extend my gratitude to her for the long-term loan.

The eventual title of this book is, rather, a play on the sense of malls as large monoliths that can "maul" us emotionally or psychologically. The subtitle's opening word, "deciphering," should, I hope, help to give you a sense of how this is a project that unfolded via slow research. As I gradually felt the contours of what shopping in Canada might look like from a cultural standpoint, the feeling that I was sleuthing my way through something complex and a bit hidden kept returning to me. My deciphering is, of course, only one such type: as a gerund, the verb indicates the ways that this search is an ongoing one, and I invite you to take it on as well.

—

After walking some more around Chinook, I take a seat behind the cordoned-off area where Santa's workshop sits. Now that Christmas is over, the workshop is waiting to be dismantled and put into storage for next year. I'm following the lead of others who have already transgressed against the rope designed halfheartedly to keep us out of this space. Once that line has been transgressed, the space becomes a free-for-all. Several children scramble up to Santa's empty chair. I expect that security guards will be along before too long in order to shoo us away. In the meantime, this chair that I'm in, which was probably installed here for parents waiting while their kids visited with the jolly old elf himself, is pretty comfortable.

Security in malls tends to make me jumpy. It is likely that my jumpiness has to do with my response to security and policing in general in the West's post-9/11, War on Terror environment, but it's specific, too, to the way in which the mall is a private space that acts as though it is a public one (more on that in the chapters to come). The reduction of freedoms and possibilities in Chinook Centre is pretty much at the whims of whoever owns the space (in this case, as usual, one of a few large corporations that own most malls in Canada: Cadillac Fairview). Sure, I've seen the film *Paul Blart: Mall Cop*, and I know that mall security is more or less powerless. Nevertheless, the space between legal and permitted behaviour in malls always gives me pause.

Santa's workshop is a pretty sad affair. I have to admit that I don't like Santa, though, so my bias is showing. Yes, I know that my dislike of Santa is controversial. But there you have it. I've tried to get over it, with mixed results, ever since I became a father. A short ramp leads up to Santa's seat, on the front of a false sleigh. The sleigh is housed in a sort of cheap-looking house-slash-workshop. Cotton stands in for snow, while about a dozen pines – real potted ones – are scattered around, with multi-coloured lights and balls decorating them. More kids run up to check out Santa's chair.

While I've participated in the Santa ritual in the past, I don't think that I've ever really understood it. Although I'm not Christian, I've grown up in a loosely Christian context and celebrate the sort of mostly secular Christmas that many white people in Canada do. I remember, as a child, going to Lansdowne Centre in Richmond, BC, to visit Santa. How is it that we maintain this strange and even cruel fiction? He hardly seems a benevolent chap: he surveils children's behaviour all year long and then metes out rewards or punishment according to his assessment. What constitutes "good" and "bad" behaviour is only ever defined by inference and by cultural norms, rather than with any specificity. And, of course, Santa runs a sweatshop of enslaved elves. Happy elves, but a sweatshop nonetheless. When I was younger, I was fascinated by the way in which Santa seemed to come straight out of the nineteenth century as a sort of perfect capitalist: he maximizes labour efficiency and has a flawless supply chain, given his magical delivery system. He is a Dickensian industrialist in reverse, or Marx's nicer doppelgänger (he even shares the same beard). In contemporary culture, however, he seems to me to be an increasingly malevolent figure of watchfulness and monitoring (especially when you throw in that Elf on the Shelf® product, but don't get me started on that). Yet kids appear to like him well enough. Though I suspect that my elder daughter, who is eight as I write these words, is at this point mostly humouring us and her younger sister. She's clever and has almost certainly figured out who the man behind the curtain is on this one.

Sitting in Santa's workshop now that he and his elves have returned to the North Pole (in order to start working on next year's perfect delivery) does change the mood here. Sunlight streams in through a skylight. Children are running up and down the ramp and climbing on the sleigh. Adults are making various use of the space. The rules that applied until the twenty-fourth of December are no longer in force. We are free – or at least freer – to make use of the space as we choose. Santa Claus and his army of disciplinary elves are out of the picture for now, even though (as always) he may be watching. The cameras are, anyhow; I spot at least one.

People walk past, carrying growing numbers of bags. I've added some things to my haul too: the most recent Giller Prize–winning novel and some heavily discounted, non-denominational holiday cards (for the late ones that we always end up sending). The bookstore was another good example of how shopping pre-determines and reduces our choices from the get-go. That shop is a "bookstore" in which less than half the space – true of most of their locations – is taken up with books. More of the store consists of small treats, stationery and luxury-type items like blankets and candles. The range of books available is limited and appears to be shrinking.

Across from me, some kids have found beanbag chairs and are flopping merrily onto them as their parents check their mobile devices. I can't help but think about how filthy the bean-bags surely are after a month of being trodden upon by Santa's visitors. A young girl opens her mouth and then chews on one. I wince. A few chairs over, a young boy asks loudly into a phone where someone is – a question that, someone observed to me in a conversation, we never could have asked before mobile devices came along.

—

The most common comment that I hear from people when I tell them that I am writing a book about malls is a version of the following: "You know, that means that you will actually have to go to malls, right?" Anyone who knows me knows that I'm no fan of mass consumerism. Karl Marx has often, quite literally, been my bedtime reading. (He's actually quite funny sometimes.) I may choose to participate in aspects of consumer culture, but my participation has usually been reluctant or else invested with some degree of self-defensive irony. So people sagely noted to me that I seemed to be setting myself up for frustration.

However: I'm not just trying to get over the mall. I'm trying to understand it. I'm trying at least to make my peace with it. And I'm trying to imagine past it. The endeavour has been an important one for me.

—

Eventually, I retreat and head for the Chinook Bowladrome, thirty-two lanes of five-pin bowling fun. It's pretty much the only part of the mall that looks to be untouched since my childhood. I take a back seat and watch. I'm not in the mood to bowl, but I enjoy seeing the teens, the families and the kids. That said, I find bowling to be about the most frustrating sport there is. The alleys are perfectly straight, the balls are round and the pins fall right over if you hit them. How come, then, it's so difficult to hit the pins? Nevertheless, I love the enjoyment that it generates for my family. Its simplicity is also its strength and perfection.

Up in the mall, the volume of shoppers is still increasing. Corridors are operating with de facto right-of-way systems, and lineups are now out the door for many of the shops. It looks like it will be a profitable day when all is said and done. I've just had a blended juice smoothie-type beverage and a small chocolate bar to keep going. My load is heavier from my total purchases: one pair of jeans, one winter hat (the fake-furry kind, to replace a worn-out one), three pairs of men's undergarments (again, replacements), that book and that one box of atheistic Christmas cards (a paradox, you might point out). As the day wears on, I watch folks carting televisions and other large-scale purchases out of the mall. None of that for me today.

On the lanes ahead of me, balls hit the hardwood and roll toward the pins. For the most part, amateur families are bowling, but further over there are a couple of serious-looking men bowling by themselves. The décor here is gaudy, neon and pastel colours on geometric designs. This bowling alley has been here for long enough that it has come back into fashion; the paint has been freshened up and there is a comforting cheekiness in its style. Rock from the 1980s and '90s thrums in the background, and alley workers are spraying down the shoes. The carpets look surprisingly clean and the kitchen isn't busy. Maybe a third of the lanes are occupied.

Upstairs, in the mall proper, the crowds will swell until the mall closes at eight p.m. I'm done though. I've indulged in my more-or-less-annual pilgrimage – or my Dante-esque descent into the underworld of consumerism – and I have the luxury of being able to head home. It has, in fact, been a fun day, one that I've enjoyed. The Despair never really materialized, although I glimpsed it once or twice. I suspect that it was held at bay because I came in order to write as well as to shop; the two held each other in balance.

A new family has just started bowling. A four-year-old boy has rolled his ball as slowly as you can imagine toward the pins and, at length, knocked a couple of them over. The slow speed, though, has meant that the lane's computer system didn't record the ball, and now the pins are stuck. Someone will have to fix it. But the boy is overjoyed at seeing the pins topple and that, for the moment, is all that matters.

The Mall vs. the Outdoors:
CrossIron Mills

I used to boycott so many things. I used to boycott meat. I sort of boycotted new leather products. Microsoft. Toxic things, things that were bad for the environment. I used to have a spreadsheet devoted to all of the different boycotts. Conrad Black and all related Postmedia products. Things manufactured in sweatshops. Products from the Gap. Nike, absolutely, and ditto Amazon. Things that weren't ethically sourced (though the meaning of that word – "ethically" – was always a bit of a shaky one). Things not made by unions, especially when I was more active as a labour organizer. Blood diamonds (not that diamonds were at all within my price bracket). I was generally more concerned with making positive consumer choices whenever possible. In that spirit, I would choose items that were manufactured within Canada when possible. I definitely chose union-made articles when I could. I tried to avoid products like unnecessary electronics because of the heavy metals and coltan mining associated with those. I supported local foods. Culturally, I avoided particular artists or writers or musicians who were thought to be misogynists, racists or homophobes and supported those who voiced what I believed were progressive perspectives.

These days, I have to confess that I make many of my choices based upon my own judgments rather than the judgments of others; I try to be slower to judge and to work first of all from a place of forgiveness. My same values are all in place, but expediency is a big factor too. I have been in a hurry for the last few years, but I still do what I can. I will choose organics over conventional agriculture, domestic products when possible to cut down on shipping and union-made if there is a choice. However, my time management has been such that I, too, often end up making quick decisions over "correct" ones, in part because there can be a certain arbitrariness to boycotting products. Boycotting can, at times, be very useful – I think of the boycotts of South African products during apartheid – and it can, at other times, become one of those things that I beat myself up over, to little effect. As with Oscar Wilde's critique of charity – that it ends up enabling the fundamental exploitations of capitalism to continue unchecked – I question consumption-based activism. At my most cynical, I see it as a form of slacktivism more attuned to appearances than actions, not too different from clicking a "like" button to support whatever protest movement, or else hashtagging a social sentiment in order to feel good about oneself. If I'm still shopping, then I have a hard time believing that anything fundamental is changing anytime soon. So, instead, I try to valorize the good decisions that I am able to make and I strive, above all else, to be compassionate with myself. I find that I am better off not berating myself over having sometimes shopped at the Gap. I feel like there has been a diminishment of the possible choices in the world, which makes me sad; I suspect that I am part of both the problem and the solution. I'm well aware that

I'm bargaining with myself, and that part of that argument is that the overall good that I might do in the world can outweigh the consumption-based bad. But I'm painfully aware that all of these rationalizations do very little, really, to promote or create social or political change.

Oh, and I used to boycott Walmart and McDonald's too. More on that to come

———

CrossIron Mills is a newer mall, opened just outside of Calgary in the rural district of Rocky View County, at the edge of the town of Balzac and adjacent to Highway 2, the main artery that connects Edmonton, Calgary and places in between. This mall is, as will come as no surprise, a place that celebrates consumption and capital, but I find it to be a very weird one – weird enough that I'm going to ask you to allow me to stick with my home province of Alberta for the moment. The reason that I find this mall so strange is that, alongside it being a place of consumption, it is also a place that simultaneously celebrates rural culture and signals its disappearance. One of the key places at which we see this culture disappearing is at an ecological level, and this mall has a great deal to say about ecology. While the developer was careful in thinking through elements of the ecological impact of a shopping mall of this sort, the mall is destructive of the prairie topsoil on which it was built – and more. The resources that I see being of particular tension in this case are water and oil, though, rather than soil, and so I will pursue those in this chapter while thinking about rural cowboy culture and its celebration and disappearance.

But most importantly, when I walk through CrossIron Mills, I see a mall that is highly, highly self-aware. In my reading of the space, this mall demonstrates a lot of irony in its celebration of consumption, a sort of tongue-in-cheek knowingness that displays and incorporates its own critique. That the mall is so self-aware should give us pause: one of the main things that I hope comes across in this book is that, to return to that point in my introduction, it is simply not enough to view shoppers and merchants as enshrouded by false consciousness. In many of the activist movements in which I have participated over the years, this was one of our greatest weaknesses: I've often believed, consciously or not, that people do "bad" things – like shop mindlessly and exploitatively – because they aren't aware that what they are doing is "bad," or contributing to sweatshops, or contributing to greenhouse gas emissions or whatever. That if we could just educate people better, they would act differently. It's one of the challenges of "consciousness raising" politics.

There is of course tremendous benefit in education; if I didn't believe that, then I wouldn't be writing this book or doing most of the things that I do. CrossIron Mills, though, suggests that developers know what they are doing, and this mall pushes me to realize that my fellow humans know, more or less, what they are doing too. The false consciousness thesis is just not enough: there is a lot more complexity to the situation of shopping than simply denouncing it as bad and having people wake up and see the light. We are all living in compromised positions (heck, just by being privileged enough to read and write we live with the compromise of knowing that we have access to literacy, something that is denied to millions but that is within our collective power to change). What CrossIron Mills teaches me, alongside its ironic narratives of resource exploitation, ecological destruction and mourning the loss of a piece of Western culture, is just how very imperfectly human the strange act of shopping is.

Shortly after CrossIron Mills opened – it opened in stages, between roughly 2009 and 2012 – the Calgary-based poet Weyman Chan wrote a poem called "sweeter than unbaptized hair," a poem with the subtitle "after five hours shopping at CrossIron Mills, Balzac." In this poem, the speaker, seemingly worn out from a day's shopping and contemplating death as "a precise art," suggests that "hope does seem ascetic one day / Byzantine the next."[1] I like this sentiment because it captures some of the complexity of how we decide to see the world. While hope, that troublesome notion, might seem to require asceticism – a strictly anti-consumerist sense of self and purpose, alongside the sorts of restraint that we might associate with ascetics – this same notion can suddenly seem "Byzantine" the next day. This term is useful because of its multiple meanings: first of all, we might think of the complex tracery of the art forms of the early medieval Byzantine empire, which are wonderfully hopeful at their best. But we might, too, think of the adjectival use of the term to describe bureaucracies: for hope to be Byzantine is for it to be lost beneath a mountain of paperwork or other detritus – like that of the mall. The complex, Byzantine mall, in other words, can be a place of hope, but it can also leave us searching for its ascetic opposite, a space of quiet, solitude and remove in which we might breathe and relax. Hope, that complex desire, is difficult to pin down: it is multiform, and whether we feel hopeful or its opposite, despairing – The Despair – can depend very much upon things as fickle as our moods. After having travelled to CrossIron Mills several times myself, I can sympathize entirely with what Weyman Chan conveys in his poem.

———

CrossIron Mills, built and managed by the Canadian company Ivanhoé Cambridge (based in Montreal), is not dissimilar to other North American indoor malls and, in particular, Vaughan Mills in Ontario, on which it is partly modelled. It is the largest single-storey mall in Alberta, with close to 1.2 million leasable square feet. It is organized according to "neighbourhoods," each of which features a different theme: fashion, ranch, resources, fossils, entertainment and sport. I'm not sure how that medley of disparate themes was chosen. The décor of each section embeds the themes throughout, while the stores, when the mall's leases were originally drawn up, seemed to me to be loosely organized to reflect these themes. In addition to the movie theatre and entertainment complex, the other marquee attraction is the Bass Pro Shops retail outlet, which takes up nearly ten per cent of the leasable space. This store, which claims to be founded upon principles of natural conservation, specializes in selling outdoor equipment like guns and fishing tackle. It contains a small pond that is stocked with the sorts of fish that one might catch in the Alberta wilds. It also contains over one hundred and fifty taxidermied animals. I stood in one corner of the store and counted until I couldn't bear to keep going anymore; I could have kept going well above one hundred and fifty.

The other important feature of CrossIron Mills is the massive expanse of the parking lots. With over six thousand parking stalls, the asphalt outside highlights the fact that this mall is not built in an urban environment at all. Similar to many of the malls built from the postwar period to the present, it is a mall built far from the homes of the people who shop there. Or, rather, it is a mall that is built in the expectation of suburban growth, with the parking lots ready to receive everyone from neighbouring communities that are yet to be built. As the website for the mall celebrates, "the gravel required to complete the roads and the parking lots required a dump truck every three minutes for 10 hours per day for 100 straight days." When I was doing my initial research, it was impossible to get to the mall without access to a privately owned vehicle, although there was a shuttle available for mall employees (for a fare).[2] The mall's initial motto, "You are so worth the trip," highlights the difficulty of getting to the mall in the first place (they have used a variety of different mottos and advertising catchphrases since). The parking lots are enormous, sprawling under the prairie sky that I love. As much as I want to understand and forgive human behaviour, for I too am far from perfect, these parking lots are hard for me to take.

So I have to admit that I am very much predisposed to dislike this mall, for all of the reasons that you might expect from an urbanoid with rural roots like myself: sprawling parking lots, mandated oil consumption, ruined prairie lands and, of course, the shopping. When I read them, at least to me, the mall's claims for social responsibility ring rather hollow. "Environmental consciousness" is highlighted as one of their "pillars of community investment" in the "Commitment to Community" page on its website (I might reply: What community? The mall is deliberately built outside of Calgary, Balzac and Airdrie in a rural district; these neighbourhoods-to-come are still a ways off).[3] Although the mall harvests rainwater from the roof into cisterns for irrigating their outdoor landscaping, many of the gestures that the mall makes toward ecological sustainability seem to me to be comparatively minor. While it isn't insignificant, for instance, that the mall's roof is white, thereby reducing air conditioning needs in the summertime, the giant black parking lots divert rain from the water table and, of course, the mall's air conditioning needs are greater than those of the less-developed prairie that existed on the site previously. The mall's overall destruction of arable land and its remote location demonstrate the relatively small contribution that the mall's ecological gestures can make. I wonder if "environmental consciousness" simply means a consciousness about what the mall is doing to the environment. (Though perhaps that is just cynicism on my part. Many of my same criticisms could be applied to any shopping destination.)

But it turns out that there is much more to this mall than I realize at first. When I enter the mall, I see it according to Calgary-based writer and public intellectual Aritha van Herk and her take on the province in her book *Mavericks: An Incorrigible History of Alberta*. In her book, van Herk asserts that Alberta and its people have been and are governed by a maverick mindset, one that prompts people to act first and ask questions later. While I might quibble with the sweep of her generalizations (generalizations that demonstrate, in turn, a maverick in action), her idea of the maverick is a useful explanation of the oddity of life in some parts of Alberta. The mindset, which van Herk sees as pervasive, allows Albertans to take risks and to make space for change. She puts it as follows: "Albertans are mavericks, people who step out of bounds, refuse to do as we are told, take risks, and then laugh when we fall down and hit the ground. We know our own abilities and failures only too well, and we are perfectly aware of how often we shoot ourselves in the foot. We just bandage our toes and limp on."[4] I'm reminded of a family story on my partner's side, a rollicking, large, Catholic Métis family. Her great-grandfather was out one day chopping wood in Skull Creek, Saskatchewan (a place that no longer exists except as a dot on some maps); one swing of the axe missed and he chopped off several toes. Rather than crying out in pain, he simply said "brown sugar" in lieu of swearing, as was his wont. Then, addressing his daughter (my partner's grandmother), who was a child at the time, he said, "Audrey, go fetch your mother." He lost the toes, but limped on. The non-swear of saying "brown sugar" lives on in the family. Maybe it's a prairie thing, bigger than Alberta.

But van Herk argues that it's particular to those of us in and near the foothills and eastern slopes of the Rockies. "Albertans are enigmatic," she states, and "full of contradictions."[5] For van Herk, Calgary, the main target audience of CrossIron Mills, embodies the maverick in its boom-and-bust cycles, and in its oil barons (the city is of course in a bust right now as I write this, to which I'll return in the conclusion). She argues that the city, from early on, has had "a massive inferiority complex, making it all the more determined to prosper and grow and beat the world at its own game."[6] The city and what are now becoming its exurban bedroom communities – nearby towns like Airdrie to the north, Cochrane to the west, Okotoks to the south and Strathmore to the east – indeed seem to be poised for endless growth, expanding ever toward the horizon and into farmland. There is little to prevent the spread and ongoing embiggening of Alberta's largest city.

CrossIron Mills, in many ways, embodies the maverick mindset – and also demonstrates many of what van Herk sees as the frustrating, contradictory aspects of it. It says one thing and seems to do another without much apparent concern for consistency. For instance, it promises sustainability while being situated in an unsustainable location; it promotes the reduction of consumption while providing opportunities for shopping; and, as I'll suggest in just a moment, it celebrates the Albertan figure of the cowboy while permanently altering the ranchlands of the province, heralding the cowboy's shadowy disappearance back into the unknown from which he usually enters in those Western films that I grew up watching.

—

The cowboy's shadowy figure looms large in the "ranch" neighbourhood of CrossIron Mills. This section of the mall is a celebration of an absence: the mall is built on what were formerly four quarter sections of ranchland (a quarter section being 160 acres). In the ranch neighbourhood, we see a large outline of a cowboy, easily ten metres tall, dominating a pedestrian junction. This sculpture of the cowboy's outline towers over a pretend fire that resembles a cookout. Down one of the corridors from this junction, we see, up above the shops on ground level, reproductions of false fronts of stores from early western settlements. These ones in the mall, simulations of the original false fronts, are one further step removed: they are false false fronts. These ersatz false fronts, rendered in a muted palette so as not to overwhelm the colours of the "real" stores below, suggest a sort of historical progression. Once there were small-town main streets, with general stores and saloons; today, the mall has way more of the same to offer us. These false false fronts, above today's stores, suggest the continuity of shopping, its shifts from ranch time (which is consigned to the past) to the present, and, in doing so, suggest that people in Alberta have shifted their patterns of consumption over time – but have still continued the overall pattern of buying stuff.

But at the same time, there is more going on here, and I find myself coming up with a subtly ironic reading. What if these false fronts from the early prairie stores have been purposely reconstructed here in order to suggest the similar falseness of today's stores? That is, the false fronts of early prairie stores were built in order to deliberately exaggerate the stature of those stores, making them seem taller than they were. Bringing false fronts into today's mall suggests that the same logic of aggrandizement and falsehood can be applied to the new shops below. Moreover, CrossIron Mills' historical nod to these false fronts signals a keen awareness that the shops in the contemporary mall are also destined for the historical dustbin. As the owners' leases expire and the stores move on (as some did as early as right after the mall's initial Christmastime shopping season), the new stores too will prove to be transient and false.

These false fronts bring me to one of the books that I have taught many times: Sinclair Ross' landmark 1941 novel, *As For Me and My House*. Ross' book is often held up as marking the "beginning" of prairie fiction in Canada; it is a novel that makes continual reference to small prairie towns with similarly false-fronted stores along their main streets. In fact, the false fronts are one of the main motifs of this novel about isolation within prairie communities, and the demands of conformity that small towns can make upon those who live in them. The main character of the novel, Mrs. Bentley (we never learn her first name), sees these false-fronted edifices as a personal insult. "False fronts ought to be laughed at, never understood or pitied," she states early on, describing such stores as "smug."[7] Mrs. Bentley's husband, Philip, is in the habit of sketching small-town main streets, and she interprets the differences from one sketch to the next as being emblematic of his shifting mindset. In one of his images, for example, she notices that "the false fronts . . . stare at each other across the street as into mirrors of themselves, absorbed in their own reflections."[8] She provides, through Philip's art, insights into how inward-looking small towns can be, how mean-spirited those towns' judgments of their inhabitants and how alienated, ultimately, anyone is who does not fit in perfectly (as she and Philip pointedly do not).

Those false fronts are not just incidental to *As For Me and My House*: they take their toll. "Three little false-fronted towns before this one," Mrs. Bentley remarks, "have taught me to erect a false front of my own, live my own life, keep myself intact."[9] She suggests that life on the Prairies is full of falsehoods, full of people who appear outwardly as though they match the life scripts that are presented to them while, inside, there is much more turmoil – as, indeed, there is for her. She notes that time is passing, that she is aging, and she says that she and Philip are old enough in their lives that "it's not enough to put a false front up and live ... behind it."[10] She is, in other words, dissatisfied, and so is Philip. The false fronts have held them back, or, more specifically, Mrs. Bentley suggests, "these false-fronted little towns have been holding us together, nothing else."[11] At the very end of the novel, just before the Bentleys escape to the city and leave the false fronts behind, there is a violent windstorm that quite literally brings the winds of change. One important result of the storm is that "most of the false fronts" are "blown down."[12] Although Mrs. Bentley is one of the most enigmatic characters in Canadian literature, endlessly discussed in articles and classroom essays, her views on the false fronts seem pretty clear: to her, the false fronts signal all that is wrong with the small, insular communities that she has lived in on the Prairies.

What then do we make of the false fronts of CrossIron Mills? If they show us the continuity between shopping in early prairie towns and in today's large, enclosed malls, then we are invited to view the new stores below, too, as being as mean-spirited and oppressive as the shops in Mrs. Bentley's town of Horizon. The conformity that is enforced through the false "choices" of consumption (always being prompted to ask which thing one should buy, not whether or not to buy a thing) parallels the conformity that the small towns enforce on their inhabitants in Sinclair Ross' novel. As well in the novel, differences are rooted out or else marginally accommodated through simplistic forms of choice (both Protestants and Catholics live in Horizon, for instance, although they do not much interact – and that's about as far as religious or spiritual tolerance goes in that context). Mrs. Bentley suggests that the false fronts keep our dreams in check: they keep us imagining that only so much might be possible, and the same may be said of a mall that restages these relics. But the question that remains, for me, is whether we might read these displays as holding on to some potential for an ironic reading. Maybe not quite yet, but, as I walk through the sunless, air-conditioned mall, I look for this potential in CrossIron's corridors.

———

I think that finding the irony and self-awareness of a mall like CrossIron Mills (or Chinook Centre, or any of the other sites that I discuss in this book) is important because these signal to us at least a couple of different possibilities: for instance, if mall-builders are as self-aware as I think that they are, then perhaps there is hope for changing the landscape over time. Or, alternatively, if the irony and self-awareness that I spot at moments is, in fact, cynical, then we might find another sign that, indeed, we are in deep trouble as a species. Such cynicism would signal that we know better yet still behave badly, consuming our way toward oblivion. Both of those options (and of course there could be more than just two readings of these moments of irony) are much more interesting to me than the idea that we are all just a bunch of sheep when it comes to consumption.

Another place to consider the potential for irony in CrossIron Mills is in its relationship to waterways. Water is a concern in

Alberta, as the 2013 floods in the Bow Valley displayed, and it is under threat across Canada and beyond. California, for instance, is facing unprecedented droughts as I write this, and these droughts will have effects for all of us across North America, given how much of the continent's food is produced there. We may think of Canada as having a large amount of water given our lakes and streams, but scientists caution that we should learn to think otherwise. Professor of ecology David Schindler argues that Canada's frequent "glib assurances of water abundance . . . are lies," while zoologist and water expert John Sprague finds that, even though Canadians are constantly told that we have a great deal of fresh water, Canada in fact has a very limited fresh water supply that is fully renewable. Sprague argues that "Canada appears to have lots of water, but this is because of a topography that creates a few large lakes and many shallow, small lakes, along with a cool climate and low evaporation of water. In fact, our share of the world's renewable water supply is relatively modest." In this context, Sprague recommends that Canadians rethink the "myth of abundance," a myth that, in his view, "has probably encouraged a cavalier attitude toward the use and manipulation of water within Canada and reduced the concern for environmental side-effects."[13] The Canadian belief that the environment is vast and endless, self-renewing and able to accommodate ever-growing human demands has led to a consistent neglect of the actual flows of water in the country.

In Alberta, the water management system is based upon permit allocations. This system allows, in theory, for flexible water management that is not determined solely by historical patterns.[14] The system varies across the province. For instance, an agreement with Saskatchewan requires that fifty per cent of the Oldman River's flows must remain within the river as it passes out of Alberta to its eastern neighbour. The strains on the Atha-basca River, tied to bitumen and oil in the north, are already well known.[15] As a consequence of Alberta's market-based approach, large users have to secure the rights to draw water from specific aquifers, and these users are able to trade these rights with other users. These transfers have become more important in southern Alberta after 2006, when the provincial government closed the Bow, Oldman and South Saskatchewan Rivers to new applications for withdrawals.[16] This policy change affected the development of CrossIron Mills, which was announced in 2004. The mall did not secure water rights until 2007, after a long negotiation that revealed that the mall needed as much water as the nearby town of Strath-more, which has a population of about ten thousand. The mall's attempts to secure water rights proved to be controversial, with the Alberta Liberal Party inquiring in the provincial legislature into what appeared to them to be closed-door dealings for water between politicians and developers. The City of Calgary ended up refusing to extend water rights for the development, as the mall lies just outside of city boundaries. The challenge was finally settled when rural residents of the Western Irrigation District agreed to sell some of their existing water rights to the town of Balzac and to the mall for fifteen million dollars.[17] The permit allocation system proved itself to be tricky, and the negotiations demonstrated precisely how controversial a resource water can be.

This issue of Albertan water allocations and the politics of water show up perhaps best in another book, Cherokee writer Thomas King's 1993 novel *Green Grass, Running Water*, which has also long been a critical favourite in Canadian universities. While King's novel predates the more recent model of rights management in Alberta, one of the reasons that critics have flowed toward this novel is that it demonstrates some of the issues connected to who has access to water and why.[18] The novel's focus on water parallels the case of Milton Born with a Tooth, a man from the Peigan Nation who spent time in prison for his actions in resisting the development of the Oldman River Dam in 1990. Another Albertan maverick, Robert Kroetsch, reflecting on that dam in his non-fiction book *Alberta*, notes that "the demand for water, agricultural, industrial, recreation, urban, are relentlessly on the increase; the supply that flows down off the eastern slope of the Rockies remains fixed." Moreover, Kroetsch states, "the environment is under pressure, and with it the varieties of life that, over the past century, over the previous thousands of years, over the preceding millions of years, shaped themselves to fit that environment."[19] In King's novel, the right to water is equally tied to the right to land, as a development company, Duplessis International Associates, seeks to build a massive dam that infringes upon the lands of the Blackfoot people. The dam appears slated to go ahead until Eli Stands Alone, a retired English professor, secures an injunction against the dam. (It is also possible that professional critics – English professors – like this novel because Eli is, more or less, a hero in the action.) The legal battle continues throughout the novel, with the developers strategically hiring Blackfoot lawyer Charlie Looking Bear as their front man. They send the project overseer, Clifford Sifton, to visit Eli on a daily basis to ask him to relinquish his rights to the land immediately below the dam. Sifton avows that dams "don't have politics" in his speech and his actions, but as the book goes on that claim is continuously undercut by the tensions between Indigenous folks and white settlers.[20]

Water runs throughout the novel. It bubbles to the surface all of the time. The title itself refers to the idea embedded within treaty discourse that the treaties were made for all time, for "as long as the grass is green and the waters run," a phrase that gets repeated throughout the novel as well.[21] The dam, however, impedes this water – the waters cease to run. One character observes to Eli that the dam, which has been built but remains inoperative as long as Eli's injunctions continue, has already damaged the land downstream: as a result of the failure of the annual floods, the cottonwood trees are in danger of dying, deaths that in turn imperil the ability of the Blackfoot to use these trees in the Sun Dance.[22] The novel's resolution – if it can be called a resolution – can only arrive through the mischief of the trickster Coyote, who oversees the destruction of the dam in an unexplained earthquake (and with the help of three equally unexplained floating cars). The earthquake destroys both the dam and Eli's home downstream, and claims Eli as its victim. The importance of water and the appropriate stewardship of the land are made abundantly clear in the novel, as readers are told that "environmental concerns," "questions about possible fault lines under the dam" and "Native land claims" were all set aside by regulators once the dam's construction begins.[23] That said, the exact significance of the water is up to King's readers to explain; Coyote notes at one point that "all this water imagery must mean something," but the novel does not provide us with any direct or too-easy answers.[24]

Yet water clearly has not only ecological but also political ramifications, based upon who has access to it and who does not. These issues surface in the architecture of CrossIron Mills, though not quite as I might expect. The resources section of the mall features for the most part agricultural and industrial imagery, like imagery of wheat shafts, wind turbines and oil. Water does not feature prominently here. It seems at first glance that, in celebrating the resources of Alberta, the one resource that proved most controversial for the mall's development has been downplayed. However, things seem different when I head to the food court. There, the high ceilings display images of Alberta's past and present, set around the edges of its semicircular design. When I look underfoot, all of a sudden I find water. Not actual water, but tile work that represents waterways. These cascades of blue tiles stretch across the food court, under the tables and feet of shoppers resting and eating. I notice that, at each of the pillars that hold up the roof, a small plaque describes a different waterway. And here, again, I spot a trace of irony. The mall, built upon the open prairie, of course displaces or buries minor waterways: there are rivulets that feed into sloughs, sloughs that feed into streams and brooks, and streams and brooks that feed into rivers and lakes everywhere. But these have disappeared in the mall, replaced by the tiles underfoot. The food court becomes a giant map – it is very large – of disappeared water, of paths that have been displaced either underground or diverted elsewhere. The recording of these paths across the food court signals a seeming awareness that something has been lost in the construction of the mall – or, even, that the mall itself participates in, and is part of, disassembling the very sorts of Albertan ways of life that it also wishes to celebrate (as with the cowboy and the outdoor cookout). Water, this complicated resource and likely source of future political tensions in southern Alberta, is flagged for us in its very absence.

—

Let's go back for a moment to the resources neighbourhood, and from there cross over to the fossils one. The discourse around resources in Alberta and Canada – and globally – is impossibly complex, and I will happily recommend Naomi Klein's book *This*

Changes Everything as a great place to do some in-depth thinking about these issues in a way that meshes with my own views.[25] One other writer whom I have found provocative on the subject of the environment – and on oil specifically – is an academic named Allan Stoekl, who has written about "postsustainability," a notion that we can think about when looking at CrossIron Mills. Sustainability, which is often a term that we find ourselves turning to when discussing environmental initiatives, is a flawed idea, Stoekl argues. He instead wants to embrace, as he puts it, a postsustainable society "in which we labour to expend, not to conserve." He points out that every time we burn any amount of oil, we do something unsustainable, because oil is a finite resource. That much we know, but Stoekl turns the conventional logic on its head: perhaps the idea of sustainability is in fact the wrong one, because it is necessary that we consume. Even our lives are, in the end, unsustainable: we will all use up our own resources – our aliveness, if you will – and we will die. And so, at a certain point, the goal is not to sustain ourselves forever, but instead to consume the time that we have in mindful ways. So, for Stoekl, "the problem becomes how best to expend" our time, our lives and our resources.[26] When we look at it that way, it might become easier to see that our current mode of consumption – business as usual – is not a particularly good one. Resource consumption then becomes something more like an existential issue and, in a surprising sort of way – at least to me – Stoekl's rejection of sustainability becomes a deeply ecological argument. As he puts it, "we are destroying the environment just so we can drive those gas guzzlers on six-lane highways to the strip mall."[27] Sociologist and philosopher Zygmunt Bauman puts it similarly when he argues that "the consumerist society has to rely on *excess* and *waste*."[28] If, however, we attempt to think postsustainably, or, rather, if we try to become conscious of the expenditures that we choose to make, then perhaps some different possibilities open up. Instead of simply trying to avoid all expenditure and consumption – because to do so is, ultimately, to die (and I choose to affirm life while it lasts) – we find ourselves having to make choices.

What does this thinking mean for the resource and fossil neighbourhoods at CrossIron Mills? The resources neighbour-hood, I already noted, features imagery associated with many different industries. The most notable, surely, is the oil industry, that famous and notorious industry in Alberta associated with greenhouse gas emissions, controversial pipelines, the befoul-ing of waterways – as well as wealth and jobs (like, for instance, the oil royalties that, in part, fund the provincial coffers that in turn fund the university that in turn pays my day-to-day salary). How oil appears in CrossIron Mills is notable: in the middle of the resources neighbourhood, there is a pretend oil derrick with wheels that children can crank in order to force mock oil from its top. Or, at least, I assume that it is mock oil. It looks black and sticky from afar, but it is contained behind clear acrylic tubes. What does this installation of chrome, clear tubes and black oil teach us? For the kids who run by and crank its silvery wheels, it is, on the one hand, simply a way for kids to blow off steam (itself a loaded expression). But it also suggests that oil is fun, that sucking oil up from underground is an entertaining diversion and pastime. At the same time, the placement of this derrick, right in the middle of the passageway, reminds us of oil's central place in the Albertan imaginary. The other resources – the wheat shafts, the windmills – tend to be placed either high overhead or on the walls, giving some scenery and backdrop. They do not interrupt the flow of one's stroll through the mall. Oil, however, stops us in our tracks: we get to interact with it; we get to account for it. It is, in Albertan terms, the current centrepiece of the economy and of the culture of resources. And, as we are implicitly being told with this installation, it is also fun! We can play with it, we can manipulate it, and it is all in good jest. There is, yet again, something ironic at play here, but I find the irony to be just a little bit elusive. I can't quite pin it down. While I am observing this installation, children run up, laughing, spinning cranks and enjoying themselves as the oil spurts up above. I instead find myself befuddled, trying to get the joke. I suppose that it is a postsustainable one: we are deciding what we are going to consume. Frankly, I don't like many of the decisions that we have been making in Alberta, although, from my political side of the coin, I am cautiously optimistic these days. We are deciding to consume, and maybe we are beginning to do so with an awareness that oil is what we are choosing to consume when we decide to do so – and that we could make better choices. Perhaps that awareness will lead to us making those better choices in the future, or even in the present.

—

Maybe I'm just looking for it, and maybe I'm belabouring the point, but I can't shake the feeling that there is indeed something deeply ironic about CrossIron Mills when I arrive at the fossils neighbourhood. I take my cue from Linda Hutcheon, who writes in part about Canadian irony. She writes that "the country that gave the world the Rhinoceros Party can prove that it has a fine sense of irony."[29] When I round a corner in the mall and enter into the fossils neighbourhood, I'm no longer doubting it: this mall is intentionally ironic. There's no other way to identify it, try as I might. I confirm this suspicion while looking at an installation near the food court. It is unattributed; I look in vain for a little plaque or tag. This installation is a stack of rectangular shapes, each enclosed in a wire mesh. Each layer contains different items designed to evoke archaeological strata. The lower layers consist of pieces of shale rock, evoking ancient, prehistoric times. As I move my gaze upward, I see that each layer depicts more and more "recent" events. One layer, around the middle, contains evidence of Indigenous history; another consists of evidence of colonial contact, featuring a document from the Department of Indian Affairs and other miscellanea. While this historical curtailing of Indigenous bodies is troubling, evidence (yet again) of the narrative of the "vanishing Indian" – a narrative against which many in Indigenous studies have written and protested – my eye is caught by the topmost layer of this fake archaeology. This layer is filled with the sorts of things that one might purchase, right now or in very recent history, in the mall, things like ball caps and Nintendo controllers. The top layer demonstrates, in other words, that everything the mall contains is, itself, detritus, bound to be just one more layer in history (and a pretty sorry layer at that). The stuff that I might go and purchase today is already relegated by this installation to the status of being just so much rubbish. Weird. But of course true: what I might buy today will one day be discarded, will end up in a landfill – or, at best, be recycled – becoming another archaeological layer from the anthropocene, the era when humans dominated the planet.

Is this installation proposing an ironic take on the mall? Is the mall knowingly saying to us "buy this item!" all the while being aware that it really means "this item is already consigned to the wastebasket of history"? I think that it is possible, perhaps, to have it both ways, to read the installation as both earnest and ironic.

It is possible that, before we've even bought them, consigning today's new goods from the mall to the midden of history, to be unearthed by future archaeologists, is a form of loss. These things are all going to be lost, going to be searched for in the future as evidence of a civilization that once existed. But I cannot deny the irony: the new is already garbage, and what is fancy right now is also already the déclassé junk of the future. The mall is self-aware, and it knowingly sells us stuff that we do not need and that it knows we will discard. It sells us the revolution in Che Guevara T-shirts and posters. It is aware that we are made to consciously decide to consume: there is nothing false about it, and we know what we do, give or take. This installation in the fossils neighbourhood is just one further sign that while we're aware of many good reasons not to buy new Nike shoes, we do so anyways (well, okay, I still boycott Nike, but I am wearing Adidas shoes as I write this sentence). I find myself, in the end, coming back to Aritha van Herk's understanding of what Alberta is all about: the mall wants to have it both ways, to be both ironic and sincere, and it is, as such, contradictory. But then so too is the culture of consumerism writ large: the mall and the culture of capitalism manages, as so often it does, to outstrip our critical vocabularies. The mall is unsustainable, and it knows it: it celebrates its very own consumerist, excessive self in this monument to loss, to archaeology and to the past, present and future.

Bewildered, I walk back through the mall, overtop buried waterways, and out the exit (once I find it). I locate my car in the sea of vehicles parked atop the asphalt, paved on top of a prairie paradise of ranchlands and cowboys, of the Cree and Blackfoot people of Treaty 7 and of the Métis people – and of buffalo herds that are long gone. I head home along with thousands of other drivers, and I ponder: To what extent do we know precisely what it is that we do when we shop? Has advertising hoodwinked us as much as psychology studies suggest, or are we as perfectly conscious as CrossIron Mills implies? I think that the irony strongly suggests the latter, but I need more confirmation.

No Way Out:
Eaton Centre vs. Honest Ed's

Eaton Centre, naturally, began as an extension of Eaton's department stores, one of the dominant Canadian retailers for most of the twentieth century. At one point, those of a certain age will remember, Eaton's was huge. Folks just coming into adulthood today, though, have no living memory of this increasingly forgotten store. Toronto's Eaton Centre hearkens back to the rise of department stores themselves, a rise that took place in the nineteenth and early twentieth centuries. We can take a look, for instance, at Émile Zola's 1883 novel *The Ladies' Paradise*, one of the first books set in a department store, to track some of the changes that these stores created. In Zola's novel, we see the rise of the department store in Paris. The novel uses a fictional store, the Paradise, as a stand-in for Le Bon Marché, which rose to prominence in the 1870s and '80s. *The Ladies Paradise* is, on the one hand, a sentimental novel of romantic intrigue between Mouret, the owner of the store, and Denise Baudu, one of his employees. This narrative is full of the daily drama of life in the store.

At the same time, the novel records many of the views popularly held about the rise of large stores that set about their goal of selling a little bit of everything. And, moreover, the store is, even if indirectly, subsidized through backroom deals that lead to real estate growth and shop improvements. Many people are suspicious of the store. One manufacturer says that the department stores are "just machines for exploiting people," and indeed both customers and employees are treated with a large measure of indifference so long as the money flows. But the exploitation is more specific than that: for Mouret, the store is designed, in particular, for "the exploitation of Woman."[1] Mouret deliberately designs a situation in which women jostle one another for social position through commerce and conspicuous consumption. He increases the speed with which sales occur and at which fashions turn over so that the women of Paris are caught in cycles of perpetual shopping and spending. By the end of the novel, Mouret is humanized by Denise as the two find a way to overcome their class and power differences, but the underlying philosophy of the department store remains unchanged and unchallenged: it wins out utterly over the older stores that specialized in specific items.

Zola's depiction was reflected in thinking on both sides of the Atlantic. During the course of my reading for this project, I came across an old book from 1932 by Godfrey M. Lebhar entitled *The Chain Store – Boon or Bane?* Lebhar, who identifies himself as the editor of the periodical *Chain Store Age*, and who nevertheless claims to wish to examine the issue in good faith, examines a shift in the United States toward larger, more centralized chain stores. The chain store is often seen as an outgrowth or refinement of the department store, or as its next logical step. So Lebhar is concerned for the most part with what we would identify today as both department stores and chain stores, which he subsumes under the label of "a method of distribution involving the use of more than one retail outlet." He notes a great deal of anxiety in the United States about the rise of a more concentrated retailing system, which he records across multiple levels of society. The concerns are reminiscent of those in Zola's novel: old ways of doing business are being destroyed, small business owners are being put out of work, wages are being cut, communities are being undermined and what Lebhar perceives as moral degradation looms on all sides. Although Lebhar sticks more or less to the economic side of things, a sense of moral panic is observable in many of the sources that he quotes. Ultimately, and after much discussion, he concludes that "the economies of distribution" offered by the chain store "represent the single greatest contribution . . . so far developed" toward eradicating poverty, and that "its economic advantages alone provide its social justification" as a harbinger of "social as well as economic progress."[2] So much for a balanced view. What is most interesting about a study like Lebhar's is not the accuracy of his grandiose claims – the claim of eradicating poverty, for instance, comes off as rather far-fetched, especially given the increase in income disparity in North America and globally since the 1970s (at least). Rather, what I find interesting is the strongly defensive posture that Lebhar assumes, one not at all dissimilar to the posture adopted these days by, for instance, apologists for Walmart (on which, see my discussion of the Walmart in Whitehorse below). As a society, it seems that we are profoundly concerned about the ways in which we shop, about the moral and social, as well as economic, impacts upon our lives – and we have been concerned for a long time.

We cannot, however, simply rely upon French and American starting points when we think about a place like Eaton Centre in Toronto. Canada's history of shopping is a unique combination of European and American concerns that are blended by the history of the fur trade and beyond. Take Eaton's, a uniquely Canadian store: there are still Eaton Centres today in Toronto and Montreal. Victoria, Vancouver, Calgary, Edmonton and Winnipeg all had places called Eaton Centre in the past. In Canada, such chain department stores take us into a deeper history, a history connected to the colonial "origins" of this country (origins only from a settler-colonial perspective, that is). The Hudson's Bay Company is still active as a department store, for all of its ups and downs, including its current American ownership. The North West Company, the Bay's former rival, can still be traced through to the Northern/NorthMart stores in Canada's northern communities today. We can say, quite literally, that the forerunners to department stores colonized Canada during the period of the fur trade.[3] And so I realize that we need to add another dimension to the story as we set out to try and figure out what Toronto's Eaton Centre is about, before I bring it into conversation, in turn, with Honest Ed's, as well as the Dufferin Mall.

———

When I make one of my not-so-infrequent trips to Toronto, it is late November. I am there to visit friends. I love Toronto, deeply, even if that isn't always a popular sentiment in other parts of Canada. Toronto was the city of my mixed-up twenties, the city in which I completed my final university degree, and the city in which I more fully became an adult. It was the city in which my older daughter was born, a home birth in a wee condominium unit that overlooked the intersection of Queen and Spadina. I love many things about Toronto: its sheer mix and collision of humans from every corner of the Earth, its public transit, its jumbled yet nevertheless confident sense of itself, its lake, its river, its smells and, oh yes, its malls. I still have a number of very close friends in Toronto, even though many of us who studied together at university have moved to new cities.

This late November day, my destination is Eaton Centre. It's a fascinating place. I decide to walk there. My friends' place borders on Trinity Bellwoods Park, so my walk takes me along hip, trendy Queen Street West, right past where I used to live. How clean you have become, Toronto! Everyone in the city seems beautiful to me these days, in a particular well-coiffed sort of way (tied to exactly which parts of the city I find myself in). I wonder if consumption patterns are changing here: Does living in very small, precise condominiums mean that Torontonians are spending their incomes on fewer, nicer things because space is at a premium? When I lived in Toronto, much of that time was spent in a rundown, very wonderful old house in the Annex, before we moved to our own wee condo. I used to find Toronto to be dirty, cramped, old and musty. I was often woken up, in our first place, by the sound of crashing and smashing bottles as the strip club across the street emptied out the previous night's detritus into a recycling bin. I loved the grittiness of the city, and I used to love shopping in the very mixed stores of Kensington Market, where I could easily meet most of my needs.

These days, Kensington is moving upmarket – gentrifying is the term that most folks use. I was myself a part of this wave of gentrification, as a well-educated professional and writer, which is something that I'd like to be sure to take into account: many (although of course not all) of the people who decry gentrification are themselves caught in the challenge of being linked to those very processes, which I think many writers are increasingly coming to realize; the articles that I read on the topic seem to be pretty self-aware. But Toronto's take on life seems so shiny now – so clean! The new streetcars and subways gleam along (even if, thank goodness, they still have the same smell), while the steel-and-glass condominium towers, so many of which have been added since I moved away, gleam up into the sky. The new smells on the streets these days are mostly espressos and cosmetics. Everyone looks so well put together. I pause on the streets and can't help but wonder at the new sorts of normativities – new ideas of what a "normal" life should look like – that all of this beauty is generating, if not enforcing, upon everyone.

My walk along Queen Street West is certainly a case in point. It is a thoroughfare for hipsters. A block of the street near where we used to live burned down not long before we moved away, and that whole stretch is now more or less made up of boutique clothing stores, yoga studios and coffee shops. Some of the old places remain; I stop in at Come As You Are, an anti-capitalist feminist sex toy co-operative, and I have a chat with the person working there (who is very good at quickly saying "anti-capitalist feminist co-operative").[4] Further on, some old haunts remain – the Horseshoe Tavern, the Rivoli – but lots of the stores are new ones that arrived after I moved away. I keep heading east, seeing patches of the old brick buildings – some of which are falling out of use – all backdropped by looming new towers that look like they are made out of Lego bricks. I fight back my nostalgia and my resistance to how the city is changing, and hope to see it with a curious rather than critical eye. I cross Nathan Phillips Square, pause at the new, oversized TORONTO letters that border the wintertime skating rink, which is shortly to open for the season, and then walk on, plunging into Eaton Centre at the Queen Street entrance.

—

The history of department stores is, in many ways, a microcosm of the history of Canada. From Indigenous trappers trading at colonial outposts to images of Métis voyageurs, much of the colonial encounter was driven by the fur trade. The pace of the trade, in turn, was driven by the two companies vying for land, market shares and royal favours. In part because the companies have tended to keep quite good archives, they have been subject to plenty of studies over the years. Prior to 1821, when the North West Company and the Hudson's Bay Company formally merged, the competition between those two companies shaped much of what the modern geography of Canada would look like. The fur trade, in particular, drove this period of colonization: weirdly, Canada would not look like itself – heck, it might not even exist as such – if wealthy Europeans hadn't been so very keen on wearing shiny hats made out of beavers.

Late in the nineteenth century, the Hudson's Bay Company, as well as what remained of the North West Company, began to look more toward the distribution and sale of goods rather than their production. In 1869, the Hudson's Bay Company sold what was then known as Rupert's Land to the government of Canada (a problematic sale when looked at today from an Indigenous perspective). Amounting to nearly a quarter of North America's landmass, the sale was a huge transfer, and it forestalled American interests in the region. The sale then led to the numbered treaties with Indigenous peoples, from 1871 onward, as the government of Canada began to administer the region (such as Treaty 7, which governs the land on which I live). The sale of Rupert's Land would have – continues to have – a profound effect upon Canada, upon settlement and upon the Indigenous peoples whose lands were transferred by pen and by capital from one set of foreign colonizers to another.

This period of time also coincides with the beginning of the rise of department stores in Canada, which consolidated themselves into the early twentieth century. Eaton's is the most notable of these, but others like Simpson's, Woodward's, Simons, Ogilvy and so on made their marks upon different local geographies. By virtue of selling in large, centralized stores that were destinations for shoppers travelling to city cores, department stores held immense sway in the rise and development of Canadian urban spaces. At one point, for instance, Eaton's alone employed eleven per cent of Canada's workforce.[5] Its main warehouse and distribution centre in Toronto spanned several blocks of downtown space, along Yonge Street, from Queen Street up to College Street. As the company moved into the west in the early twentieth century, its Winnipeg store became one of that city's most notable downtown establishments (today, it's where the Bell MTS Place is, the home of the NHL's Winnipeg Jets). All across Canada, department stores became organizing forces of cities, and of how Canadians colonizing the western provinces lived and shopped.

Canadians, of course, didn't only shop in physical stores. Eaton's distribution was also marked by their mail-order catalogue, those old catalogues that kids apparently used to strap to their legs and use as shin pads while playing pond hockey (I say "apparently" because that was before my time). Catalogue distribution was very successful for Eaton's for many years, and the catalogues themselves are an important component of Canadian retail history.[6] Other retailers used similar means of distributing their goods to people farther away from the main urban department stores; we always had the Sears catalogue around when I was a kid. Although the landscape of retail has changed a great deal in the interim, it is fair to say that Canadian cities would be radically different places without stores like Eaton's having shaped their early downtowns.

—

When I enter Toronto's Eaton Centre, I am struck immediately by the press of humans inside, by the holiday decorations that brighten up the space and by Michael Snow's well-known sculpture, *Flight Stop*, perhaps better known as "those Canada geese that you see in Eaton Centre." I didn't care too much for the sculpture in the past, but I've come to recognize and appreciate its importance. It is very well staged in the main galleria of the mall, with the light coming in from above. Working with the north-south axis of the mall, the installation consists of a collection of geese that appear to be coming in for a landing at the mall's south entrance. Each individual goose is sculpted from a series of photographic images, and collectively they express very well the motions of flight.[7] Suspended by wires from the glass-and-steel framing above, the sculpture achieves a surprising juxtaposition, of fowl that are wildly out of place in the midst of the throng of mall-goers. It is easily missed, or observed just in passing, but it is also a well-recognized and iconic work of art.

Flight Stop is also interesting because it is, I've learned over the course of this project, a legal precedent–setting piece of art. At one point in the early 1980s, the folks who ran Eaton Centre decided to dress up the geese for the holidays, festooning each with a jolly little bowtie to celebrate the Christmas season. Michael Snow sued the owners for defacing his artwork, asserting his moral rights over the piece. He won, in a case that established artists' continual moral and intellectual rights to their works.[8] The case led to some later tweaks in Canada's copyright legislation.

I am hungry by the time that I arrive. I look along the gallery and, peering down a floor, spy a new place to get food, a place that calls itself the Richtree Natural Market Restaurants complex – a glorified and fancified food court, in other words. I enter, get lunch and sit down. I try to face as few television screens as possible, but there is nevertheless a large screen above me, on which highlights from yesterday's NHL games are repeating over and over while I eat. As has been the norm recently, the Habs are struggling along and the Leafs are losing. Eventually, I get up and decide to go.

—

Toronto's Eaton Centre might be held up as one of the obvious examples of postmodern mall architecture. In his landmark book *Postmodernism: Or, The Cultural Logic of Late Capitalism* – a book that for many defined what postmodernism was – Fredric Jameson twice mentions Toronto's Eaton Centre. He does so as he discusses how postmodernism uses loose quotations of earlier forms, evoking both continuity with and rupture from the past.[9] Postmodernism in architecture can be defined in a variety of ways, but Jameson's writing allows us to see this architecture as, at a minimum, relying upon mixed references to older types of buildings while, at the same time, appearing to be complete, self-contained spaces. This self-containment is a microcosm of the logic of late capitalism, a logic that avers that there is no way out of anything like "the system." Eaton Centre is just such a projection of a total world (Jameson calls it a "total space"): when you stand within the mall, looking along the galleria from *Flight Stop* toward the north, there are no entrances or exits to be seen. There is no way out (okay, there are entrances and exits, but they are discreetly placed and out of the way, just like at other post-modern malls). The high glass ceiling overhead, in its vault work, references earlier European forms – in particular the arcades of nineteenth-century Paris. Looking at the mall today, some twenty-five-plus years after Jameson's *Postmodernism*, there is something distinctly post-postmodern feeling about the fact that the Eaton's brand has long since disappeared, while the mall itself still bears its name. (During the period of high postmodernism in literary studies, we might have called this effect "palimpsestic.")

Department stores, academics and historians have argued, began to lose ground in the postwar world of the 1950s. They were displaced, the argument runs, by regional malls that were havens for the automobile, a convenient luxury that became available on a widespread basis after the Second World War and with the expansion of the suburbs (expansions designed along car-friendly lines). Once everyone had cars – everyone with enough money to buy one, that is – suburban malls began to make sense in a new way. Victor Gruen, often hailed as the first designer of the modern mall, who was designing his malls for the US environment, recognized this change. His plans included blueprints for re-engineering downtown Fort Worth, Texas, into a massive mall-slash-office centre surrounded by huge parking lots – plans that were never realized.[10] In this brave new world, people became less likely to travel to department stores located in urban centres – just as they became less interested in travelling to city cores themselves, leading to all of the challenges faced by the down-towns of almost every city in North America in the mid-to-late twentieth century. Catalogue distribution fell off too as regional malls became more accessible for people with cars.

Those who have studied the decline of department stores in more depth have sought to understand how individual stores fared in this changing environment, and have, overall, suggested that intransigence and a failure to adapt led to the closure of many – most – of the department stores that, in Canada, had picked up where the fur trade had left off. While the Hudson's Bay Company survives as an important retail force, the others are mostly gone. We might argue that US retailers like Walmart cut out the working-class segment of department stores' shoppers, and look toward the changes of the era ushered in with the 1988 Canada–United States Free Trade Agreement, later superseded by NAFTA in 1994. We might argue that consumption has changed in many surprising ways that we couldn't have foreseen. Box store havens on the edges of cities, in turn, are challenging what used to be suburban malls, many of which are now in fact comparatively centrally located. Online shopping is forcing changes elsewhere, and the ways in which we shop are in flux. Eaton Centre, given its centrality in Toronto, persists and seems to thrive, but the north end of the mall, where Eaton's used to be, became home to a Sears for many years after Sears bought out what was left of Eaton's in the 1990s, after its long decline. Today Sears is embattled and has closed in Eaton Centre; the space has recently reopened as a branch of the high-end US retailer Nordstrom.

—

I decide to take on Eaton Centre one floor at a time. I start at the top floor (not counting the offices on the upper floors, even higher above us puny shoppers). The top floor of the mall is for the most part made up of higher-end clothing stores. I step into a few, fingering goods that I can't really afford. There is a large, two-storey location of a major bookstore chain, and I wander inside for a look, checking out the books and household comestibles. I nearly buy a book, but then decide that I can get it from an independent store later on (in fact, I find a used copy at a bookstore just off Yonge Street that same day). There is a display of adult colouring books – a trend at that moment that I think is fantastic (I love colouring with my daughters) – and the store is jammed with people buying mugs, trinkets, stationery, doodads and even books. Wandering out of the store, I look up at the galleria overhead, the arched glass ceiling letting in a great deal of muted sunlight.

I step outside, through a side entrance not visible from the main promenade: too much capitalism and too many beautiful, shiny people. I need a break. At the northwest corner of the mall, just a few feet from the mall doors, lies a church, the Church of the Holy Trinity, built in 1847. While it is a noble building, it is utterly dwarfed by the Eaton Centre. I notice that the church has a small memorial to the deaths of homeless people next to its door. Many of the dead are recorded simply as John or Jane Doe. I step inside, where I discover a progressive, activist church that provides sanctuary to refugees and a space for the homeless to come in out of the cold. It is a kind space, a barrel-vaulted building (running east-west, as one would expect, and thus perpendicular to Eaton Centre). It is decorated in what I might describe as an arts-and-crafts-inspired or Victorian style, though nineteenth century design is not my forte. Today, the pews are pushed to the edges of the worn, wide-cut wood floors. In one corner, a group of people who appear to be homeless are chatting. A rainbow banner tells me "Every day is pride day at Holy Trinity"; another demands "social justice now!" I tell the woman who is greeting visitors that I have passed this place for years without entering, and she says, "Well, it's about time then!" I ask for a quiet corner to sit down and find a free pew along the wall. Light comes in through the stained glass windows. It's so close to Eaton Centre that there is a clear conversation going on between the two buildings. The organ in the church lies silent, but visitors trickle in and out as I sit.

The contrast between the two buildings couldn't be any more stark. Voices, conversations, carry the length of the largely empty church. The atmosphere is calm, quiet and peaceful. That this edifice seems so very tiny next to the temple to consumption next door, of course, says a great deal about our contemporary society.[11] I have, of late, been involved with a group of people who are sponsoring a refugee family from Syria to come to Canada. We have been told that we need to raise about $27,000 for this sponsorship to go ahead, and we arrived at our goal through the collaborative efforts of about thirty people. I think of the $2,000 coats that I was just looking at in the mall and realize that purchasing one such coat is close to ten per cent of the cost of providing refuge to a desperate family fleeing warfare or persecution. Across from me, two people, by coincidence, now turn to discussing Syria. Across the aisle, a bearded man falls off a pew, then stretches out on the floor and falls back asleep. I am struck by the contrast between the affluence next door and the poverty here. That we could, as a society, buy ten or a dozen fewer coats and provide a new life to an entire family gives me an important check on those consumerist urges from which I never quite escape. But every decision bears consequences and responsibilities; as a father, I am, every day, learning that lesson more and more as I strive to become the best – though necessarily and importantly flawed – person that I can be, for my daughters and for the future.

As I leave the church, I thank the woman for making the space available, and I pause again at the memorial to homeless deaths and ponder my own privileges and advantages. Toronto seems to average about twenty-five to thirty homeless deaths per year, sometimes many more.

—

If Eaton Centre marks the high end – of at least the middle end (Yorkville, these days, caters to much of the high urban end) – in contrast to the poverty evident in the church just next door, then we also need to think about other spaces: those that are accessible for the less-than-wealthy. Take, for instance, Honest Ed's. Created by Ed Mirvish, an immigrant with a classic rags-to-riches story, Honest Ed's for years sat at the corner of Bloor and Bathurst streets, an anchor of Toronto's Annex neighbourhood.[12] I still have a bright red polyester tie that I got there for five dollars in my twenties, to wear to a drag show organized by some of my housemates. Although its demolition began in 2017, it has been an honoured, block-long Toronto mainstay since the middle of the twentieth century. It was the perfect place to shop for extremely cheap housewares, dental services, legal and immigration services, and plaster busts of Elvis. Here is what Pico Iyer had to say about it back in 2000, in the travel book *The Global Soul*:

> When I arrived at the place, hectic with carnival slogans and handwritten signs all over its exterior – WHITE SLICED BREAD 29¢; 900 GRAM BAG OF WHOLE GREEN PEAS 39¢ – its turnstiles were already spinning with customers early on a Sunday morning (sometimes, I'd been told, there were traffic jams at 4:00 a.m. around the discount palace, in honor of one of its all-night sales). Virtually every square inch of window space, on all the walls that looked out onto the street, was plastered with old newspaper clippings and yellowed photographs reciting the legend of "Honest Ed." Immigrants everywhere are the ones who run stores for other immigrants, in a kind

of oral tradition whereby yesterday's newcomer knows exactly what today's or tomorrow's will need (international phone cards, tax advice, pieces of luggage, and tickets home); what Mirvish seemed to be offering was a version of the classic immigrant tale – the American dream – with Canadian trimmings.[13]

While this passage is, on the one hand, a bit bombastic, on the other it is a rather accurate portrait of Honest Ed's, a place that was perhaps best understood as a site of gaudy excess. Everything was dirt cheap, and you could get pretty much everything there that you needed to survive life in Toronto, all under one roof.

Iyer doesn't note, though, that Honest Ed's was also frequented by students from nearby campuses, like that of the University of Toronto – as I was when I shopped there in my twenties. There is an important difference, though, which is that many of the students were able to afford more expensive stores (their student loans would be paid off later, seemed to be the thinking), unlike those who were recent arrivals to Toronto and relied upon the cheap canned foods in the basement grocery section and on the bargains on clothes suitable for work. I think that it was that mix of twentysomething students and newcomers from the world over that led to the unusual mix of Elvis busts and affordable suits. Everyone who wanted to save a buck was served at Honest Ed's – even if that buck being saved was, for some, a bit tongue-in-cheek, or just a way-station on the road to a likely middle-class future (for which, *mea maxima culpa*).

It's because of this unusual mix of things that it makes perfect sense that, in the third book of the graphic novel series Scott Pilgrim, *Scott Pilgrim & the Infinite Sadness*, by Bryan Lee O'Malley, Scott fights Ramona Flowers' evil ex-boyfriend Todd in

Honest Ed's. The Scott Pilgrim series of anime-inspired books, set in Toronto, follow the rather hopeless and clueless young Scott as he learns from his foibles. In a quest to get over his own past relationships, in which he failed to be a supportive or caring guy, and in order to become the boyfriend of the mysterious – and American – Ramona, Scott has to prove himself in a series of fights against her evil exes. The film adaptation of the books, starring Michael Cera in the role of Scott Pilgrim, unabashedly uses Toronto locations throughout, such as Casa Loma and the Pizza Pizza on Bloor Street at Bathurst (with Honest Ed's visible through the windows in the background).

A key scene that the film removes, however, is the fight in Honest Ed's. Todd, who is the bass player in a cooler band than that in which Scott plays bass, is now dating Envy, one of Scott's own exes (she is the lead singer of the band Todd is in). Todd is evil and has superpowers because he is a vegan. As Todd and Scott enter the store to begin to duel, the clatter and clash of juxtaposed goods terrify young Scott Pilgrim. Todd emerges with a weapon made of a mishmash of household goods sold in the store, and Scott, in a desperate attempt to survive, dons pads and sunglasses from the shop. It is Todd, however, who caves in, his psychic vegan superpowers, running on high gear, overwhelming him and leading to the store's sudden collapse. Both survive and will have to duel again. (Eventually, Scott wins after the vegan police revoke Todd's superpowers for having eaten chicken.)

What is significant to me in this sequence of events is the role that Honest Ed's plays. When O'Malley first brings the store into the book, a text panel provides an image of the store, its opening hours, and then notes that there is no explaining the place ("Explanation: None," the panel reads).[14] It was a place of inexplicable combinations, of everything that one needed, assembled under

From *Scott Pilgrim & The Infinite Sadness* © 2006 Bryan Lee O'Malley, published by Oni Press.

bizarre, text-heavy, retro signage that was, unto itself, a very uniquely Torontonian experience. The destruction of the store in the comic book mirrors, or foreshadows, the real-life destruction of the store, except that the store's true demise, at the hands of condo developers, is way less cool than the way it went down in Scott Pilgrim.

—

I return to Eaton Centre and descend to the second floor, and stroll from the north end of the mall at Dundas Street back south toward Queen. Eaton Centre, although it does connect, via both the underground PATH system and above-ground corridors, to other, more complex, buildings, is itself easy to navigate – a long north-south gallery of consumption. I hit the south end, then drop down another floor and double back to the north. The lower I go, the more affordable the stores become, though nothing here is exactly working class – there are no Walmarts or Dollar Stores (at least not right now). The bargains improve as I descend, but they are not as good as they were at Honest Ed's. I am struck by how many of the stores grew out of clothiers and fur traders. The desire/want/need for new textiles continues to drive so much of consumption in this age of fast fashion, and clothing is clearly the backbone of today's Eaton Centre.

When I hit the north end again, I head to the basement, which connects to the subway, where I pass through the main food court and by a sporting goods store. This basement is done in tile work with very clean lines and thoughtfully placed soft lighting. It is very busy and I struggle to find a place to sit down and write these words. This food court has the usual mix of restaurant chains, but I am also surprised to see a place called Urban Herbivore. It is either the namesake or a second location of a place I sometimes used to eat at in Kensington Market. They made great yam and date muffins. The logo is different, and it feels weird to see it in the mall, but they have similar muffins, though these feel more mass-produced. That's the cost of growing a business, I suppose.

This food court is also where, in June of 2012, there was a shooting that left two people dead and five wounded.[15] There don't seem to be any traces left of that event today, but I think for a moment about how quickly a peaceful, bustling scene like this one could turn to mayhem. I also remember another shooting, the 2005 Boxing Day shooting on Yonge Street, very near here, that happened when I lived in Toronto – a shooting that left fifteen-year-old Jane Creba dead after having been caught in a crossfire.[16] Mall security walks by and I spy a telltale surveillance camera overhead, something that we have all become more or less accustomed to in the years since 9/11 (with varying degrees of acceptance). Beautiful people wearing mostly black and grey clothing walk past me with phones in hand, trays of food held in their other hands, purchases in bags suspended from their wrists. The people here represent the four corners of the Earth. In their peaceful unison they are, I hope, a sign that we aren't on a path of complete self-destruction.

—

But Eaton Centre represents only a certain tier of the Earth's corners – it caters, it's worth emphasizing, to consumers with relatively high levels of disposable income. As such, it sits in sharp contrast not only with Honest Ed's but also with more local or community malls like the Dufferin Mall. Dufferin Mall is, in itself, not all that interesting. When it appears in Scott Pilgrim – in the fourth book of the series, *Scott Pilgrim Gets It Together* – that's more or less how it's introduced: as "not a particularly exciting mall."[17] It proves to be a nice enough, everyday space in which Scott and his friends can wander, over in the west end of central Toronto. It has Dollar Stores and a Walmart. It's just like any other shopping space (also increasingly unlike, say, Toronto's Yorkdale Mall, which has been pushing for high- and higher-end status over the past few years, perhaps most recently visible in their Fashion Santa campaign during the 2015 holiday season, in which Santa was no longer a portly Victorian gentleman but a leather-clad hip old dude[18]). Dufferin is an accessible, affordable space, one that might enter into cultural consciousness, but only on the periphery of our vision.

It's malls like this one, though, that are significant in cities across Canada for how they respond to the immediate needs of those who live in their neighbourhoods. Dufferin has been perceived as being at times troubled by, among other things, "youth gangs" and the drug trade. Writing for the Caledon Institute of Social Policy in 1997, then-mall manager David Hall examined ways to make the Dufferin Mall a "true urban centre" for youths and shoppers in the aftermath of several violent incidents in the mall. The mall opened up a learning resource centre for the three thousand or so youths who visited the mall daily, created a retail services learning strategy to get them involved in the mall itself, and sought links with religious and theatre groups. Hall notes that malls are what he calls an "anomaly" as privately owned spaces used by the public.[19] (As per one of my arguments that runs throughout this book, I differ from this line of thought and see malls as a part of the long-running privatization of public and common spaces, and perhaps as the most visible site of that tension in urban environments). The need to incorporate public services into a mall like the Dufferin Mall demonstrates part of what we lose when we give up on public spaces. Eaton Centre is a big, downtown mall that is less immediately embedded in a community. That the services in Dufferin Mall are now embedded within the logic of the private, rather than private spaces being lodged within a greater public sphere, is, in my view, an important thing to observe. The mall, the not-particularly interesting mall, is a place where we come together to shop, but now it's also where we come to learn and to experience culture: one of the changes that Dufferin experimented with was a community theatre in the mall, as one more means of engaging and including youths in a mall-based urban community. The cacophony of varied demands and needs in the mall points us in a mix of directions as baffling as the signage at Honest Ed's.

—

After I leave Eaton Centre, I exit to Yonge-Dundas Square, where I end up making a donation to Black History Month and am also asked for money for the Easter Seals Campaign. Yonge-Dundas is Canada's closest approximation of Times Square. Lit up with advertisements on all sides that seem to reach higher every time that I visit, it is pretty impressive. The eastern frontage of Eaton Centre looks quite tame after all of the construction nearby over the last decade. Yonge-Dundas Square is a key place for the city: I have seen concerts here, and I have protested against war here, too. I've been here many, many times. I walk north up Yonge Street, which still houses a mission and some strip clubs, but it is also way "cleaner" than it used to be. A condo building advertises itself as Canada's tallest, with penthouse suites going for over fifteen million dollars. Yes, we can call it what it is: gentrification.

As I hit College/Carleton, I turn right. College is the name of the street as it runs west of Yonge; Carleton, which I choose, runs off to the east. A friend has told me that what used to be Maple Leaf Gardens has finally reopened. It was basically derelict throughout my years in Toronto, but, up until 1999, it was the home of the storied, if for many years lacklustre, Toronto Maple Leafs (who also contribute the plural form "Leafs" to Canadian English, a grammatical oddity that I rather enjoy). The ever-growing Ryerson University has bought the building, raised the ice level up a couple of storeys, put in new athletic facilities and leased space on the ground floor to a grocery store. I go in, head up to ice level and find a seat during what turns out to be the very end of a practice for the Ryerson Rams men's hockey team. As a contrast to the makeover of the Montreal Forum, which I will discuss in the next chapter, this transition feels like a successful one: the large, well-designed grocery store is hopping when I visit; the athletic facilities are in use. There are, here and there, posters and other reminders of the Leafs – long since moved on to the Air Canada Centre near Union Station and the ever-troublesome Gardiner Expressway – but the Gardens are not trapped in a nostalgia for their storied past. The place feels alive, like it's moving on – as Toronto does in general. A few players stay behind after practice, taking long-distance slapshots. It feels like a happy place. Toronto is ever on the move: changes to the major buildings mark how people interact with their city, patterns reorganizing themselves in fascinating ways. The city's shops, streets, spaces are all studied and pored over. In the process, we learn something about how culture itself changes over time. I leave and wander on through Toronto's streets, its hustle of commerce, of lives being lived, of bodies striving and surviving and learning how to be together in a complex web of subtle daily negotiations.

Buying Memories:
The Main, the Montreal Forum and
the Underground City

It is a rainy November day and I am on my way to what used to be the Montreal Forum, which always seemed like the greatest building in hockey – a temple to the sport – during my childhood. The Montreal Canadiens left the Forum in 1996, heading to the Molson Centre (now the Bell Centre), where they still play today – and they haven't won a Stanley Cup since the move. Before the Forum, they played in a small arena on the corner of Mont-Royal and St-Urbain, which is now a grocery store in the Plateau, near the apartment that I rented with my family for the year that we were lucky enough to get to spend in Montreal during the writing of this project. These days, most of the people I speak with don't seem to remember much, if anything, about the old Forum, which I find surprising, given that it still stands. But, then again, I suppose that I'm not speaking with hockey fans, which is also only a label that I would apply to myself under the right circumstances.

I am only on my way to the Forum, however. I'm not there yet. At the moment, I am sitting on a couch in Montreal's Musée des beaux-arts on Sherbrooke Street, looking at a painting by Claude Monet. The painting is one of his many pieces executed at Giverny. This room of the gallery has work by Cézanne, Monet, Pissarro and others; the next room over has an impressive, if slightly minor, modernist assemblage of Picasso, Dalí, Léger, Braque and beyond. The museum is undergoing renovations – hammers bang in another room. An exhibition of Auguste Rodin's sculptures has just ended. I like the museum: it consists of several buildings on either side of Sherbrooke Street, all connected by underground galleries. It is a veritable maze of art, generally curated in a manner that is friendly and welcoming to the general public. I'm sure that the art world has a more nuanced view of it, but I find it to be a space in which I am very happy to spend time.

Writing about Montreal has proven to be a challenge. Yes, there are malls here: strips of box stores have popped up in the suburbs, and there are more conventional covered malls like the Rockland Centre or the rather surprisingly named Place Versailles, Montreal's oldest indoor mall, which bears no resemblance to its original and namesake outside of Paris. But the Montrealers with whom I speak claim that they don't shop in malls. It is a city of boutiques, with the streets – St-Laurent, St-Denis, Ste-Catherine and so on – animating much more of the consuming imaginary than any of the malls appear to do. I lean into the couch – a chaise lounge – and examine this piece by Monet. It is an impressionist painting, of course, and uses a palette of greens, blues and pinks that I associate with much of his oeuvre. It is an image of a tree-lined pathway that leads up to a green-shuttered house. The foliage overwhelms the viewer, and there is a balance between the orderly lines of the path and house, and the fecund abundance of the flower beds and overhanging trees. It is, ultimately, a restful work, quiet shadows tumbling across the pink gravel of the pathway up to the house's door.[1]

When I arrived in Montreal, one of my colleagues, over espressos, suggested to me that he finds the city to be one of different rhythms than those to which I might be accustomed. It is a city that calls for a different approach to many aspects of living. Some of the things in this city are maddeningly inefficient, like the constant practice of tearing up the roads, to the point that the orange "Rue Barrée" signs are part of Montreal's iconography. Other aspects of the city are lovely, like the boutiques that line the major streets of the Plateau. Yet, culturally, the patterns and cultures here that govern how people consume seem to remain out of reach, silent and a bit mysterious, not unlike this work by Monet.

Later on, I pass through a room devoted to art produced in Quebec during the Quiet Revolution – Paul-Émile Borduas, Jean-Paul Riopelle and others – which might have been a more obvious room in which to contemplate the cultures of consumption in this place. Two young women sit in front of a Borduas canvas, their sketch pads busy. But the impressionist room has helped me, I think, to consider Montreal and Quebec more as the outsider that I very much remain, in spite of a year's living in the city. *La révolution tranquille*, while I have read about it for many years, happened before my time, and my understanding of it remains more or less academic. Watching the cultures of Quebec unfold allows me to recognize the challenges of understanding "Canadian" culture, and how much we might contest something as seemingly simple as the organization that I've used in order to write this book. Quebec also challenges the labels through which I understand literature and whether literature here participates in what, in universities at least, we call "Canadian literature."

Quebec does stand out and I understand that, for some, if not many, placing it into the category of "Canadian" is something that rankles, not entirely dissimilar to how the category does for many people in Indigenous communities as well. I step out of the museum and head, face-forward, into that set of thorny issues.

—

When I began to consider the cultures of consumption in Quebec, I thought first of some of the old, obvious places in which I've encountered this province. Take, for instance, the old chestnut, Roch Carrier's children's book *The Hockey Sweater*. This book, richly illustrated by Sheldon Cohen and translated by Sheila Fischman into English, is one of the now-classic books of Canadian children's literature. It was also made into a well-known National Film Board of Canada animated short film in 1980, with Carrier reading the narrative and the title shortened to just *The Sweater*.[2] In the narrative, Carrier recounts his childhood disgrace in the small town of Sainte-Justine, southeast of Quebec City. His disgrace occurs when, after wearing out his old Montreal Canadiens hockey sweater, his mother sends away for a new one through Eaton's mail-order service. As a result of a horrifying mistake, the Carrier family receives a Toronto Maple Leafs sweater instead. (Another hockey-related piece of Canadian English: they are called hockey sweaters, not jerseys, in this northern climate, as Don Cherry would be the first to tell you.) While young Roch realizes the fate that will befall him if he is seen at the local rink wearing it, his mother forces it upon him, not wishing to offend Mr. Eaton by sending it back. He goes down to the rink, the only kid not wearing the red number nine of Maurice Richard (which, my daughter pointed out to me when we watched the film together, must have made for confusing games – how did they tell their teams apart?). He is shunned, left on the bench and, when he tries to get on the ice, is promptly penalized. You really just can't wear a Leafs sweater in rural Quebec, not if you want to fit in.

The narrative is a brief one, an anecdote about the embarrassments of childhood and the conformity of life in a small town. It is a celebration of the Habs at the expense of the loathed Leafs, and an exploration of the childhood desire to be understood, accepted and welcomed in spite of one's circumstances. Two things interest me here: first, the pervasiveness of hockey culture in the world depicted by Carrier. When I was living in Montreal during the writing of this book, every morning the CBC announcers discussed the minutiae of the Canadiens' fortunes in exhaustive detail. Other radio stations were more fervent – and critical – but the level of engagement even on the CBC struck me as very, very deep. Obsessive, really. It wasn't a great year for the Habs in the end and, frankly, the players probably could have done with less verbal dissection of their every move both on and off the rink. In *The Hockey Sweater*, we see a similar consumption of the Canadiens' every move: we are told that the only two things that everyone in the town, from young to old, universally participate in are Sunday mass and Saturday night hockey broadcasts on the radio. Consuming hockey then is one of the two pillars of local culture. The kids consume it in material ways: they all have the same hockey sweaters, and they all use the same hair product in an effort to make their hair look as glossy and fabulous as Maurice Richard's. They all have the same hockey sticks that they tape up the same way as Richard's. The culture relies upon having the right products – it relies upon shopping. When young Roch breaks his stick near the end of the narrative, it signals a further rupture from the community: not only does he no longer have the right sweater, he also no longer has a working hockey stick. He either needs to shop for new signs of his belonging or he needs to leave the rink and, metaphorically, leave the community, too.

Shopping, in turn, brings us back to Eaton's. The narrative describes it as a point of pride to shop from the Eaton's catalogue and not from the local general store. However, Carrier's mother cannot read English, and so her understanding of the catalogue is limited – she relies upon the images. When ordering the replacement hockey sweater, she pens a letter to Mr. Eaton, in French, and encloses what she hopes will be enough money. The letter is then sent to the Eaton's distribution centre in Montreal, where the horrific mistake occurs and the Leafs jersey is sent. There are several things going on here at once. First, Carrier's mother's monolingualism is seen by her son as a point of shame: she cannot handle the English of the catalogue and, rather than seeking help, she writes her letter in French instead. There is power in language, and in this case the mother is at a disadvantage. Montreal, where her letter is received, is a very linguistically mixed city, with, historically, many of the wealthy elites of the city being anglophones; nowadays, it often feels in certain parts of the city as though one doesn't speak either French or English but something in between, a constant dialogue and negotiation across languages – and there are many, many other languages spoken here as well. The scenario is, in short, comparable to what we see in Hugh MacLennan's classic novel *Two Solitudes*, in which the divide between the English and the French leads to misunderstandings on all sides. The English Mr. Eaton (or, rather, his workers) misunderstand the Carrier order, and Roch's mother misunderstands her son's need to belong to his community, as well as Mr. Eaton's business practices (for surely he would not care if they made an exchange; being able to make an exchange was an important part of Eaton's customer service). The one who suffers, in the end, is young Roch Carrier himself, humiliated and exiled from his beloved rink. The power lies with the English, with Eaton's, and their errors impact the French, specifically Roch and the small community that relies upon the mail-order service. Consuming in the "wrong" way – or, rather, being unable to consume in the "right" ways – leads to a spectacular fall from grace.

———

With Carrier's book in mind, as well as its NFB adaptation, I walk across Sherbrooke then down Atwater to find the old Forum, situated between Maisonneuve and Ste-Catherine. It is open, and it is relatively busy, though I'm not quite sure what people here are doing. I walk around, exploring the space. It is a quasi-museum to hockey – well, to the Montreal Canadiens – as well as a cinema with many screens. There is pumping, wordless, crappy music playing. On the ground level, there are a couple of stores hawking Canadiens memorabilia, as well as a Tim Hortons. I take a seat in the one remaining, repurposed section of seating from the original Forum. Seat B5, section 210, to be precise. It is set around a tile-inlaid image of centre ice, though, based on its location, I believe that it cannot be where the historical centre ice was located. Behind me, two young men are discussing the current hockey season, weighing the Habs' chances, which look pretty good at that early point in the schedule. Montrealers are incredibly passionate about their hockey. Every pub, bar and hole in the wall seems to have the game on anytime the team plays. The building is done up in Canadiens' colours: red, white and blue. The logo is visible on flags hanging down from the ceiling, on images on the walls and at centre ice. Everywhere, images of Rocket Richard, Jean Béliveau, Patrick Roy, Bob Gainey and Guy Lafleur, among many others, remind passersby of the long, hyper-masculine history of hockey in this space.

And yet, I find the Forum to be quite sad. It is a space in decline – it is a residue of a past culture, not a forward-looking or vibrant space. Even the tinny techno sounds like it is at least a decade out of date, but is presented as though it is the newest thing. The Canadiens may still be the most recent "Canadian" hockey team to win the Stanley Cup (the scare quotes indicating the fact that players on most NHL teams are often Canadian citizens, after all) – but that was nevertheless over twenty years ago, in 1993, shortly before the team moved away from this venue. Competing narratives about nationalism jostle in the back of my mind somewhere. This seat is pretty uncomfortable, as well as small. I can see why they moved.

So what makes the Forum a sad space, exactly? I suppose it's my feeling that it could either be more of a museum, or else less – that it hasn't really made up its mind, unlike the former Maple Leaf Gardens, now thoroughly revamped by its new owners. I've been told that the cinema here is failing, that its status and future are up in the air. This afternoon, the shop that sells what looks like the better hockey memorabilia – right down to certified bricks from the original Forum, before it was rebuilt – is closed. The nostalgia tied to the building itself is being slowly hawked off, bit by bit. The people here are mostly just walking through, on their way to somewhere else in the neighbourhood. Those who are seated at the tables are young students, likely from nearby Dawson College. They are clearly interested in other things, things coming in over the free wifi, which may be one of the biggest draws of the place. No one touches the vintage arcade games placed in a few spots on the ground floor; people look, instead, into the screens of their phones and laptops.

It's clear enough to me that the attempt to turn this temple of hockey – this quasi-religious space to many older Canadiens fans – into a temple of consumption has had, at best, mixed results. Although you can come and see the latest Hollywood films here, eat a meal and do a bit of shopping, it seems safe to say that Montreal culture has moved on, and so I do too. Culture and consumption mix in curious ways: now that consumption has become the priority here, something seems to be lost. However, when this place was the centre of Montreal hockey culture, I can imagine how consumption – of hockey sweaters, of beer, of snacks or of hockey paraphernalia – would have flowed.

Leaving the Forum, I cross Rue Atwater and enter a small mall, the Place Alexis Nihon. Although it is a bland place attached to a nondescript office tower, it is very busy, full of young students. Looking at the mall map, I see that the building's underground corridors lead off the map, likely to other buildings, possibly to join Montreal's RÉSO system – better known as the Underground City. I pause for a quick refuel and then plunge into the depths of the mall, planning to see how far back toward the Plateau the path might take me. Looking up at the glass ceiling, I see that it has begun to rain.

But it turns out that my hopes are false: I am mistaken. The passageway spits me up onto Rue Ste-Catherine, the city's main downtown shopping strip, ranging from strip clubs to bookstores to restaurants and clothing shops. I walk east along Ste-Catherine in the rain until I can find an entrance into the underground. I pass rundown shops, see new condo buildings going up and then hit a stretch of chain stores. I pass Ogilvy, a long-time mainstay of

Ste-Catherine and a department store unique to Quebec. Eventually, at Simons, another Québecois department store (both are focused on textiles), I find an escalator down. Once down there, I discover that I've already missed a chunk of the underground, but I stick to my homeward direction nevertheless.

Underground, I find hundreds of shoppers pressing in all directions. The basement malls extend, cavernous and subterranean. Overhead, galleries and corridors wend off in a variety of directions. The RÉSO system claims the title of the world's largest underground covered network. Developed over a number of years, the underground city is uneven, nearly derelict in some areas and thriving in others. It sounds pretty cool, like it should have stalactites and stalagmites and troglodytes – or Fraggles, all running around in their secret world – but it's kind of underwhelming: it's really just a mall and a series of corridors. I head homeward, but make plans to return as soon as I am able to do so.

———

Montreal's underground city is built below, in part, the pre-existing shopping district that runs along Ste-Catherine. When I was younger, Ste-Catherine was known not only for its department stores but also for its sex workers and its homelessness: it is a street of mixed fortunes, of the divides between English and French in Montreal and, by extension, Quebec and Canada. When I walk either underground or on the street, I am aware of this mix, of the assortment of pasts, presents and futures, all remixed by the globalizing stores and brands that make up the street today.

Against this contemporary backdrop, and while I was reading for this chapter, I encountered Jean-Claude Germain's historical description of Ste-Catherine, told from the perspective of a rider of

the old number 52 streetcar, which ran from Mont-Royal, across
the Plateau, then down St-Laurent – the Main – and then across
Ste-Catherine, bisecting the city and crossing what was once perhaps a clearer demarcation between the French and English sectors
of the city. I first encountered the description, in translation, in
the Vancouver-based *Geist* magazine, which led to a chase for the
original text. Germain describes a westbound crossing of the
section of Ste-Catherine that I've been walking across as follows:

> The procession of cinemas and department stores contin-
> ued along Ste-Catherine as far as Peel Street, whose corner
> was, according to the Anglos, "the centre of the city"....
> Now we were skirting a fashionable neighbourhood, fash-
> ionable except for a striptease club, Chez Paree, which you
> could spot in the distance on Stanley Street. On the right,
> a...market...for the rich who, whatever the season, could
> acquire for a king's ransom fruits and vegetables of whose
> existence the rest of the city was blissfully unaware;
> Ogilvy's, a large department store, very British, for those
> who couldn't afford to dress themselves on Sherbrooke
> Street at Holt Renfrew or Brisson's; Classic Little Books,
> the first store of its kind dedicated exclusively to English
> language pocket books, and a haughty Protestant church,
> arrogant and remote, which seemed to have alienated all
> its faithful.[3]

There are lots and lots of descriptions of Montreal, but I like this
one quite a bit. Germain goes on, his verve capturing an historical snapshot and cross-section of the city's commercial strips in
an era during which long-standing Catholic ways of living were
giving way to newer modes of being. The effect is one of jarring

juxtapositions: strip clubs next to high-end shopping and church spires competing with marketplaces. Montreal's streets seem not to have decided what they wish to be and so, instead, try to be all things at once. But that sentiment is not quite right. Let me try again: they are all things at once. The wax museum is in the top of the Eaton Centre, and the Hudson's Bay Company – which was once headquartered in nearby Lachine – and the Christ Church Cathedral sit comfortably right next door to one another (although if you go indoors, you can bypass the church by taking the underground corridor).

This description of Montreal's past circles me back around to other depictions of the city that I encountered while growing up – in particular, those of Mordecai Richler. When I walk up St-Laurent heading to Mile End – Fairmount, St-Viateur and Bernard Streets in particular – I encounter the world that Richler brought to life in his writing about the city. Richler is a writer whom I associate strongly with Rue St-Urbain, naturally enough given his novel *St. Urbain's Horsemen*, and he obsessively writes about the neighbourhood in which I spent my year in Montreal. Not only are the places described in his work on display today, but the city actively celebrates the writer, too. The Mile End library is now named after Richler, and Wilensky's lunch counter, a location that appears in Richler's work, has a corner devoted to him.

Descriptions of these parts of Montreal surface again and again in Richler's work. I am struck, for instance, by the following description of St-Laurent in the book *The Street*, a collection of stories:

Two streets below our own came the Main. Rich in delights, but also squalid, filthy, and hollering with stores whose wares, whether furniture or fruit, were ugly or damaged.

The signs still say FANTASTIC DISCOUNTS or FORCED TO SELL PRICES HERE, but the bargains so bitterly sought after are illusory – and perhaps they always were....

It was to the Main, once a year before the High Holidays, that I was taken for a new suit (the itch of the cheap tweed was excruciating) and shoes (with a built-in squeak). We also shopped for fruit on the Main, meat and fish, and here the important thing was to watch the man at the scales. On the Main, too, was the Chinese laundry – "Have you ever seen such hard workers?" – the Italian hat-blocker – "Tony's a good goy, you know. Against Mussolini from the very first." – and strolling French Canadian priests – "Some of them speak Hebrew now."[4]

The Main, St-Laurent, is known as the line (or one of them – they shift and move over time) that traditionally divides English Montreal from French Montréal. Richler describes his Jewish community as living just on the English side of the line, St-Urbain being two blocks over to the west. But the Main is much more than a dividing line. It is a place where Montreal's different communities collide, sometimes in strife, but more often in commerce.

_____

I walk the downtown stretches of Montreal in search of what it means to shop in this city at the level of culture; I also drive out to the malls and suburban strips. The department stores do make for a useful index, so I poke around in Ogilvy, Simons and the Bay on Ste-Catherine. I don't, however, get a sense of what it means to shop here, according to the culture of the city. The Bay is very quiet, Ogilvy more so. Simons is busy, but many of the shoppers there, and in general on that stretch of street, seem to come from elsewhere: I hear many recognizably American accents in the English spoken in the stores and out on the street. Underground, the scene feels more local, but the stores tend toward the impersonal: three food courts in a row (in Les Cours Mont-Royal, TD Place and the Complexe Les Ailes) repeat many of the same banal fast-food joints. People seem to be hurried and a bit harried. There is something very generic about this space and about most malls in general. The more time that I spend in the Underground City, the more it becomes clear to me that I need to continue to search elsewhere in order to understand what it means to consume in Montreal.

—

After circling the city for some time, I realize that I've been looking in the wrong places: the best place to look, at least for me, turns out to be quite literally the view out the back window of our small, temporary apartment on Rue Clark, just north of Avenue des Pins. Out the window, I can see, straight ahead, Rue Roy stretching to the east, and St-Laurent bisecting it. Roy ends when it hits St-Laurent, continuing on our side of the street as an alley that runs for half a block, ending at our two-storey building. When I look out that back window, which I often do – as it is in our laundry room, just off our kitchen – I see people walking up and down St-Laurent as they pass in and out of view. It's a bit of a rough street; in his biography of Mordecai Richler, M.G. Vassanji describes Clark as being the "bottom rung" of the social ladder, even back then.[5] With surprising frequency, I see men pissing in the alley just below me. Dozens of men over the year, shaking out their last drops of urine against the graffitied walls, completely visible to the walkers on the Main. Over the course of the year, the alley is closed twice because of shootings, and once I called an ambulance to attend to a woman who was blasting her mind inhaling aerosol chemicals, nearly passed out, half-hidden behind the alley's lone telephone pole.

It turns out that St-Laurent, and the Plateau more generally, is a great if challenging place to witness Montreal's shifting culture of consumption. This is the Main that Richler describes, much changed a half-century later, yet much the same in some respects. Ste-Catherine, these days, is largely composed of international chain stores and many of the shoppers are tourists (not unlike myself); St-Laurent seems to give evidence of a bit more continuity. I realize that I've been looking in the wrong places most forcefully after reading Heather O'Neill's writing. Montrealer O'Neill's first two novels, *Lullabies for Little Criminals* and *The Girl Who Was Saturday Night*, are set just beyond the men pissing in my alley – they could easily be minor characters in her work. The characters in her novels roam up and down St-Laurent and across the Plateau, with some of the action taking place down on Ste-Catherine. But their primary domain turns out to be a territory that I share for most of my year: the Plateau, from Mile End (as far up as Bernard, say) in the north, Parc to the west, Sherbrooke to the south and St-Denis or Papineau to the east. The cafés and patisseries on St-Denis and Mont-Royal are the backdrop for the everyday comings and goings of children, university students, young families, elderly residents and the urban poor (I am asked for change at least daily in both French and English). Middle-aged families seem to be the main demographic that is missing, and I am told that they tend to move to Outremont or farther out after their children reach a certain age. Several former schools in the neighbourhood have been repurposed as condominium buildings and public agencies. The stores often don't stock children's clothing, just clothes for infants, toddlers and adults. In this neighbourhood, I learn from friends and acquaintances where Leonard Cohen took his bagels when he was in town, I get to meet one of the members of Arcade Fire and I witness the patterns of how some of Montreal's urban celebrities live and move.

Heather O'Neill suggests that she writes about Montreal the way that she saw it when she was twelve years old, "not the actual physical place."[6] In another interview, she expresses a feeling that the city is hers to write about, that "the city somehow belongs to" her.[7] Whether we take her writing as a reflection of the real city or as an imaginary rendition of it, O'Neill's depictions of the Plateau resonate with some small aspects of my experience of living in it, and show one perspective of how the city's patterns of consumption generate a culture all its own. If Mordecai Richler was the writer of St-Urbain for his generation, then Heather O'Neill may be the writer of St-Laurent for mine. Living on Rue Clark, a street that runs literally between St-Urbain and St-Laurent, I spend the year bridging between the two worlds and times. St-Laurent, we learn early on from the protagonist, named Baby, in O'Neill's debut novel, *Lullabies for Little Criminals*,

> wasn't an ideal place to raise a kid. It ran right through Montreal, dividing its east and west sections. It was also the red-light district and, to me, the most beautiful section of town. The theatres where famous people used to perform in the twenties and thirties had been converted into cheap hotels and strip joints. There were always prostitutes around. They made me feel bad when I was little because

they always had beautiful high-heeled boots, while I had to wear ugly galoshes. I closed my eyes when I passed them. In general, everyone dressed like they hadn't gone home from a wedding the night before. You could go to the Salvation Army, buy a pin-striped jacket and stick a plastic flower in the lapel, and call yourself an aristocrat – everyone was living a sort of fictional existence.[8]

It is a painful yet beautiful, blissed-out and strung-out existence that O'Neill describes, the kind where people live hard, short lives and where "the neighbourhood looked the worst in the morning" because "the street was empty and there was vomit on the sidewalk."[9] The Montreal that Baby lives in doesn't involve much shopping at Ogilvy; it involves staying alive as her father, Jules, slides further and further into his heroin addiction, and as the local pimp, Alphonse, begins to take an interest in her.

O'Neill describes Montreal through the lens of a child who can still witness the magic of the world around her, and who can, like in the song "Suzanne" by Leonard Cohen, see the garbage and the flowers in the same swift breath. Even though, for Baby, the city has "the colors of a dirty aquarium that needed to have its glass cleaned,"[10] and her father's hopeless hustles – like selling old chairs at flea markets in order to feed his addiction – are ugly, there are continual flashes of brightness, splashes of beauty that jump through the horrors of the everyday. Montreal's flea markets are the sites of sudden magic tricks; St-Laurent is a site of wasted, decadent beauty.

—

In Heather O'Neill's second novel, *The Girl Who Was Saturday Night*, the ruined decadence of Montreal's downtown and Plateau come into a closer conversation with the challenges of Quebec national consciousness around the time of the second referendum in 1995. The protagonist, Nouschka, and her brother, Nicolas, are the children of a once-famous, now failed and disgraced fictional singer associated with the nationalist movement named Étienne Tremblay. They live with their grandfather in an apartment on St-Laurent. Nouschka and Nicolas experience young lives of rash acts and struggle to survive their impoverished surroundings while maintaining a rebellious smirk. Here, again, St-Laurent is a site of unusual assortments, of people who hang around smoking their cigarettes in impossible weather and who pride themselves upon their mixed wardrobes, redolent of thrift store glam. Everyone in the book has either no talent or bizarre talents, like Nouschka's father's knack for writing unusual song lyrics. Nouschka describes her education as one of dropping out of school with her brother and subsequently being "educated by second-hand paperback books and madmen on Boulevard St-Laurent."[11] When, eventually, she gets a new job at a theatre, she exclaims that she loves it because no one has ever taught her, as she puts it, "how awesome work was."[12] Having a sense of time and of purpose is something that no one has ever described to her before. These sensibilities, and so many more, remain on display along the St-Laurent that I traverse in my days in Montreal.

As the novel progresses, and as a documentary crew descends upon the Tremblay family in order to make a film about them – a film that revives all of their old demons, especially Étienne's – we see the characters interact with life in the Plateau. Nicolas is in the habit of robbing stores and gas stations, but none of them ever have "more than thirty dollars in the cash register."[13] The siblings traipse in and out of stores and restaurants, getting food – "dumplings in Chinatown," "Vietnamese takeout," "a head of lettuce" or whatever the local dépanneurs have on offer.[14] Life on St-Laurent is described as follows: "Dreaming too big was the cause of much horror on Boulevard Saint-Laurent. The street was filled with people whose dreams had gone bust. It wasn't always drugs and bad childhoods that brought them this low. It was ambition. There was a whole group of fallen Icaruses sitting under the blazing fluorescent lights at the soup kitchen. Their jackets were half blown off by the fall. They had the complexions of clowns whose cigars had just exploded."[15]

While Nicolas and Nouschka come from a famous family and were themselves childhood stars, and so are expected to inhabit a different sort of world, they too are among the fallen stars of St-Laurent. The small shops, the all-night groceries and the corner stores mean that you never have to plan your life in the Plateau, as my partner observed one day as we were walking through the neighbourhood; rather, as soon as you need something, it is there, nearby. Life on St-Laurent is set up so that you do not need to believe in the future: there is no need to plan for tomorrow's lunch because there is little practical difference between getting a sandwich when you need it and getting the ingredients in advance. If anything, the difference is that having things in advance would be less practical for Nouschka, who rarely knows where she is going to be the next day. While we, as readers, might be right to be suspicious of what critic Myra Bloom calls O'Neill's "nostalgic romanticism," as well as her take on Québecois politics – the temporary, unplanned nature of the life she depicts in the Plateau has a political resonance, in other words – O'Neill's writing nevertheless points toward aspects of life in the city that resonate with the daily walks that I've taken around the Plateau.[16]

One of the places that young Nouschka and Nicolas would have passed often in their haphazard lives is a restaurant called La Cabane, which has been on St-Laurent since 1983, just opposite Schwartz's Deli and above Rue St-Cuthbert. Although they are fictional, the siblings could easily have passed by the restaurant while the writer Gail Scott sat there writing her novel *Main Brides*, given the era of both books. Cabane is a restaurant that I visited repeatedly while living in Montreal: my host at McGill University was fond of the place, and we ate there – and raised the odd pint – on several occasions. Scott's take on St-Laurent, written shortly before the 1995 referendum – *Main Brides* was published in 1993 – reveals a different, yet still familiar reiteration of the street, the Plateau and Montreal life. Her novel is a meditation written from the perspective of Lydia, who sits in the restaurant, contemplating the people who frequent it and the passersby on St-Laurent. The Plateau, to Lydia, is similar to that described by O'Neill in her works: it is a place that she describes as "carnivalesque," with dilapidated buildings and beautiful clothing – people on the street are described as "tropes of various possibilities" – but it is also a place where sex work, violence, heroin and cocaine abound.[17] Scott seems to think of cities in ways that parallel some of my thinking in this project – for instance, her book *My Paris* takes Walter Benjamin's sprawling and unfinished *The Arcades Project* as its point of departure.[18] I find, in her writing about the Plateau and the shops along St-Laurent, a reinforcement of the experience that I have of living here, although I am aware that I maintain quite a bit of social, if not physical, distance from the poverty, alienation, addictions and challenges of the Main.

—

One of the words that my daughters learned while we were in Montreal was "whimsical." Whimsy is not a simple concept, and so we spent time figuring out which things were whimsical. Tam-Tams, the weekly drum circle / circus arts / LARPing (live action role-playing) event that takes place on Sundays in the summer at the foot of the Mount, for instance, is something that we would identify as whimsical. I heartily recommend Tam-Tams to anyone visiting Montreal, as a semi-spontaneous weekly event that goes from drumming early in the day, to drinking beer on the lawns in the afternoon, to watching jugglers with flaming torches after the light falls. Whimsical and beautiful and complicated all at once.

One night, as we walked down St-Laurent in a blizzard, we were passed by a commuter on a unicycle. My elder daughter rightly – in my view – suggested that that was an instance of whimsy. The Main manages to group so many things together: dépanneurs and all-night grocery stores for food, beer, cigarettes and bad wine; many, many homeless people; derelict shops; open shops; porn theatres; badly patched asphalt; students celebrating life at all hours; bars; cafés; brunch restaurants; higher-end eateries; vintage clothing stores (friperies, en français); the wealthy and the poor; and a whimsical store that sells unicorn skulls and taxidermied two-headed ducklings. In *The Girl Who Was Saturday Night*, Nouschka warns against Québecois culture being overwhelmed by the rest of the world – by the global flows presaged by Anglo-Canadian culture – and suggests that the end result could well be "little French-Canadian bobble-head dolls dressed in lumberjack shirts next to the polar bear clocks in the tourist shops."[19] As I walked up and down St-Laurent, my sense was that Montreal isn't at that point quite yet (although it may well be if you only look down in the Old Town): on the Main, the whimsy is alive and well, with an edge of long-held dereliction and decrepitude. I learned not only of my own inadequacy in understanding what it means to consume in Montreal: I learned equally that the stories of shopping and consumerism are manifold, sometimes celebratory, sometimes reviled – and always more unpredictable than I imagined. The unicyclist stopped and balanced at the traffic light and then headed south, into the darkness and the driving snow. The last thing that we saw was the small red tail light attached to the unicycle's seat, receding into the night.

In the Middle: Shopping

I like being inside malls more than I ever used to. I used to walk into malls and instantly feel queasy, a certain churning in my guts that, in combination with the sickly fluorescent lighting overhead, would lead to headaches soon after and, in turn, to a very grumpy sort of mood. The Despair, in other words. I must say that I was insufferable in the mall when I was a kid. I don't know how my parents tolerated taking me there.

It was the 1980s and '90s when my parents were dragging me to malls. I hated Chuck E. Cheese's and Toys "R" Us, but, perhaps even more than that, it was the drab browns, the teals and the neons that I couldn't handle. That awful shade of orange that everything everywhere seems to have been decorated with in the '70s and '80s, and that lingered for quite some time. The smell of stale cigarettes floating down spiritless corridors back when you could smoke in malls. But I was also one of those kids who needed to have the tags removed from their clothes because of the itch, so it wasn't just about shopping malls.

These days, I am surprised to find that I can tolerate being in malls much of the time. They've changed, and so have I. I suppose that being older has made me more tolerant, or has at least helped me to recognize that acting miserable and grumpy doesn't change a thing about malls themselves – rather, being miserable just makes me miserable and irritates those around me. So, at a minimum, and for the sake of my family and friends, it's better that I enjoy malls to the best of my ability. Part of me still wants to be not in malls, doing totally cooler things like BASE jumping on Mount Vesuvius, or taking my kids on the West Coast Trail, or doing awesome political work all of the time, or being arrested for blocking logging trucks, or spending all of my time being a really great supporter of the students I get to teach. On the other hand, I do go to malls; they are there, and I end up there sometimes. Much more often than I find myself on Mount Vesuvius. And, when I look more closely at malls, they are fabulously weird places, and human behaviour is very interesting to observe and even participate in. Sometimes I do still run out of gas, though, at which point it's best for me to leave.

The other thing that's changed is the malls themselves. The décor has been upgraded: at many malls now, everything is or will soon be in shades of white. Lighting has been reconsidered in many places too – there is natural lighting when possible in the corridors, and more diffuse fluorescents tend to point up so as to refract off the ceilings, or else halogen lights or LEDs are preferred. I experience fewer headaches, anyhow. The malls are smoke-free, of course, and just better organized. And, as I am now the core demographic (more or less) being targeted, the mall fits me better. Marketers are pretty good at what they do, resist as I might. I think, and I am surprised to discover this, that I actually do like being inside the mall. I blame this project.

Whose Malls?
Walmart in Whitehorse

I am on board an Air Canada flight en route to Whitehorse, which will be the farthest north that I've ever been. Previously, the farthest north had been Helsinki, even though my family comes from what is called "northern" Alberta (near Athabasca, which is actually somewhere around the geographic centre of the province). It is a couple of days before the summer solstice. Out the windows of the plane, the peaks of mountains poke up through massive glaciers and intermittent clouds. The plane has begun its descent and, across the aisle from me, my partner is watching something on the tiny seatback screen. I've been reading, switching between the two books that I brought along for this trip: a dusty paperback copy of Hemingway's *A Moveable Feast*, and a book about the rise of American department stores and consumer culture, *Land of Desire* by William Leach.[1] I'm looking forward to getting out of the recycled air that I've been breathing since we left Vancouver.

The mountains grow bigger as I look out to the west and the plane pitches forward. These mountains are rounder than the ones nearest to my home in Calgary, more densely treed, more glacial. They look untrammelled and clean from up here.

We are travelling to Whitehorse to visit Walmart. I have never been to a Walmart before. For a variety of reasons, I have always boycotted it. What gets termed its anti-union practices, alongside a series of class action lawsuits by female employees alleging systematic discrimination, and its just-in-time production methods, alleged to undercut the livelihoods of workers all over the world, have always made it, to me, an undesirable place to visit.[2] The academic and popular literature that I have been reading suggests to me that it is the sort of place that I should be bound to dislike, seemingly confirming my suspicions.[3] It is the sort of place that prompts The Despair, even from afar. Those who have examined Walmart closely note that it tends to have an extremely loyal, religious and conservative clientele.[4] The store has been blamed for the Walmartification of nearly everything, from manufacturing to how we live our lives, even if we do not shop there (and including, of course, the creation of that very term, Walmartification or Walmartization; the logic is necessarily a bit circular). I get it and I think that I understand. Walmart is not a corporation whose values mesh with my own, and I view it as destructive. Its place atop the global corporate food chain makes it an obvious target for contempt and derision.

This book, however, clearly calls for me to visit Walmart for the first time, in the name of balance and representation, if nothing else. And the one in Whitehorse has called me for specific reasons, as I'll share below. I take the piece of gum that my partner offers across the aisle and chew it for the last of the plane's descent while my ears pop. As we lower onto the runway, I see more and more markers of humans passing through the landscape, rearranging it, carving pieces out of hillsides in order to build this and that. We land: one rear wheel, then the other.

One of the things that I have mentioned over the course of writing this book is that the cultural record in Canada is relatively slight as far as malls and shopping are concerned. That is, in Canada, culture is not officially about malls. The story could be different in the United States. For instance, one of the clever things about Kevin Smith's 1995 film *Mallrats*, which I discussed in brief earlier, is not only is it a film set in a mall (the Eden Prairie Center Mall in Minnesota, to be exact), but it is also a film that is about the mall and is not just using the mall as a metaphor for something else. The other obvious American film to point to is George Romero's *Dawn of the Dead* from 1978, shot at the Monroeville Mall in Pennsylvania. In that case, the mall and its zombie denizens are most definitely metaphorical first and foremost – simple yet effective representatives of the mindlessness of 1970s American consumerism, which Romero critiques. The zombies walk around in a stupor, lurching along the plaza, so closely mimicking the ways in which bag-laden consumers walk around in a commodity-induced daze that the distinctions become minimal. The idea that consumers act like mindless zombies is now so commonplace that it hardly bears comment. The 2000 film *Where the Heart Is*, set in a Walmart, falls somewhere between these two films in terms of its reliance upon metaphor, creating a mise en scène in which the store can serve as a holding place to sort out the tensions of living in late capitalist culture.[5]

When we turn north of the border, spaces like Walmart do show up here and there, but we have to read carefully to notice them. For instance, in the 2015 play *Dear Johnny Deere* by Ken Cameron, we are faced with a familiar rural conundrum. In this case, the young couple, Johnny and Caroline, are struggling to keep both their farm and their marriage together somewhere on the Prairies, at the edge of a small community. The province has begun to make plans for a new highway that would run through their property and abut with that of their neighbour, MacAllister, the play's narrator. In the meantime, a smarmy city slicker named Mike has shown up to try and buy the land out from under the financially desperate Johnny and Caroline in expectation of an even bigger buyout from the province later on. The struggle is that of perseverance in the face of long odds. The situation looks bleak, and audiences (urban ones in particular) may be inclined to wonder why farming communities keep on trying. MacAllister, contemplating being bought out alongside Johnny and Caroline, sums up the situation as follows: "I bet by this point you're wondering why do I care so much? No more neighbours practically in my front lawn. I can sell too. Soon, there'll be a Walmart right where I'm standing and I'll be a rich man. I should be dancing for joy."[6]

And yet, he isn't. The familiar small-town debate of so-called progress ensues and, eventually, the province shelves the plan for the new highway and Mike is bankrupted. Johnny, Caroline and MacAllister all keep their land. Their struggles will go on, with Johnny and Caroline reconciled to their lives together for now. The reference to Walmart is a brief one, but it is a telling one, too. In small community after small community across North America, the debate has played out over whether Walmart should be welcomed into a community or shunned. The arrival of Walmart signals a certain sort of arrival for a town – a mark of its importance beyond its own boundaries. At the same time, Walmart's arrival is frequently followed, the story goes, by the shutdown of many local businesses that either feel unable to compete or else fail financially.

At other times, Walmart appears in other culturally charged ways in Canadian culture. For instance, in Thomas King's 2014 novel *The Back of the Turtle*, there is a minor character named William Church, who is a manager of a US-based Walmart. Church is described as becoming paranoid after an encounter with a "drunk Indian" in his store, a man who either threatened or was threatened by Church – there is some deliberate ambiguity.[7] Church ends up killing another Indigenous man, the father of protagonist Gabriel Quinn, who is a police officer who comes to Church's door. While the details of Church's work as a Walmart manager seem incidental to the text, I can't quite leave it at that: experiences in Walmart engender paranoia in Church, a paranoia that leads him to commit an atrocious killing with long-term consequences for many people. In what ways do Canadians hold cultural associations with Walmart that make Church's work there appropriate to the narrative? Thomas King, who is a very clever writer with a strongly anti-colonial edge, never names his characters haphazardly – or, rather, he tends to be very deliberate in how he names his characters – and Church is a loaded surname. Is attending Walmart the new church, not unlike the widespread cultural metaphor of shopping being the new opiate for the masses (this metaphor that I am working to resist throughout this book)? I think of the correlation between Walmart and religion in the United States.[8] Are the masses welcome in this new church? Perhaps only when they behave in certain ways, ways that someone like William Church expects. The breach of the codes of consumer culture, in other words, some of which are worryingly tied to skin colour and other demographic markers, is not viewed as acceptable today, as we build new ideals of "normal" behaviour into our lives by going to Walmart.

—

We drive into Whitehorse and check out the city, which is clearly in good spirits as solstice approaches. It is a Friday when we land. The guy who rents me the car asks what has brought us north. I tell him that the main purpose of the trip is to visit Walmart for this project. He looks at me quizzically at first then says, "Well, good on ya, buddy. I came up here from Ontario, and there's really nowhere to shop here. If you want a suit, you have to fly to Vancouver." He hands over the keys and wishes us a good trip, turning to the next people in line.

He exaggerated, but not by too much: Whitehorse is a small, partly industrial northern city with a warm heart and a history it wears on its sleeve for tourists to see. From the S.S. *Klondike* – a national historic site on the banks of the Yukon River – to the historical plaques along the waterfront, Whitehorse seems keen to show its past. I learn that Robert Service wrote his key poems, "The Cremation of Sam McGee" and "The Shooting of Dan McGrew," while working in the bank on 2nd and Main. It's now a branch of the CIBC. I can also well imagine Robert Kroetsch visiting the town and then dreaming up the sorts of gold-rush fever, the sheer excess that resulted in his novel *The Man From the Creeks*.[9]

We leave our dinner at around eight o'clock, the sun blazing down on us, the weather feeling, if anything, hotter than it was before. Friday night festivities seem to be getting an early start. One thing that becomes immediately and abundantly clear to me is how thoroughly southern, privileged and, frankly, wealthy I am as a visitor. As a writer with the privilege to travel north to go to a Walmart as a social curiosity, I remain a good distance from many of the local folks that we see. Lots of late model, rusting, half-broken-down pickups and SUVs run the roads, and poverty is evident. Yet the city is very welcoming: an Indigenous man high-fives me as we walk down the street, likely with a pretty high degree of irony, but still; and our host at the bed and breakfast out past the edge of town welcomes us to the Yukon with a toast and a tale about how she, like so many others, came for a visit and then never left.

In the morning, we plan to make our trip to Walmart. After ten p.m., the sun is still shining and a fox runs across the grounds of the B & B, across the gravelly undergrowth beneath the short, stalky aspens that grow up north.

—

Today is Saturday. Today is the day that I will enter a Walmart for the first time. We wake up at the B & B and eat a hearty breakfast to fortify ourselves before heading back into town. Sitting on the front porch munching smoked salmon and croissants with locally made berry jam, we see the little fox again. Our room at the B & B is actually a stand-alone double-wide trailer, set toward one corner of a five-acre lot. The trailer is decorated with wood finishing throughout, cozy furnishings and an old wood-fired stove in one corner. It also has a musty scent that takes me back to when I was a child visiting my great-grandmother's house in Edmonton. It's a particular mixture of things that I haven't smelled in at least two decades. The B & B, in other words, is decidedly unpretentious, very welcoming and precisely the right place to have stayed for this adventure.

When we pull up in the Walmart parking lot it is a sunny, warm and busy morning. As I had read before travelling here, the Whitehorse Walmart is popular with RV campers, who can park for free overnight; about fifty or so RVs are in the parking lot, coming and going. While this phenomenon is common for Walmarts in the US – partly encouraged by Walmart itself – this sight is more rare in Canada.[10] In this case, Whitehorse's location along the Alaska Highway makes it an ideal place for international travellers to stop and stock up. I expected most of them to be from the United States, but we spoke with one couple from the Netherlands who had rented an RV and were camping there, too. There is, I had been told, a local agreement in place to limit the number of RVs parked overnight to seventy, because Walmart was having a negative impact upon the several RV campgrounds that exist around town. The Walmart parking lot is huge and could likely accommodate a couple hundred RVs, which could certainly take away from business elsewhere.

A raven lands next to our small rental car in the parking lot, probably to see if we have any extra McDonald's fries or something similar to share. The raven is black, sleek and bold. It seems used to humans. We head toward the store: it's Walmart time.

Inside, I am struck first by the lighting, which is old industrial, fluorescent tubing. The ceilings are high, the flooring is scuffed and there is no Walmart greeter. This last fact is a little bit disappointing, since it is one of the clichés about the store of which I'm well aware. After a few steps we see a greeter ambling toward the door, but he has missed us, and so no great moment passes when I enter my very first Walmart. Looking up, I also notice that there are many security cameras. We are being recorded on probably ten different cameras, provided that each unblinking black eye is working. At each set of bathrooms, signs say that one must not take merchandise in.

We decide to start with a tour of the store. I am surprised to see many brands that I have never come across before, the store brands of the legions of Walmart subcontractors. It is of course important to note that Walmart is the world's largest private employer, and just behind the US and Chinese militaries – public employers – in terms of overall employment.[11] As we walk around the store, I observe that Walmart does indeed seem to have everything that one might need: from bread to fishing tackle, jerry cans, Xboxes and jeans, it is all here. I can see how Walmart has the capacity to move to town and decimate smaller, local stores.[12] While the hardware section, for instance, is minimal, it is comparable to the old hardware stores of small-town prairie main streets that I visited as a kid. If you can get your paint mixed while buying new shoes for the kids, well then, why wouldn't you? Having everything under one roof of course has major advantages – that is, after all, one of the reasons why malls were created in the first place.

We head over to the McDonald's in the front corner of the store, the only place in the building where seating is available. In one corner, a young man reads a book, an SF book judging by its cover. The McDonald's is hopping. We order a coffee and fries, and I break another boycott: I haven't eaten at a McDonald's since the aforementioned trip to Helsinki in the late 1990s. During that trip, I had the perfect Big Mac and then decided that I never needed to go back again. I then became a vegetarian for most of fourteen years, though I am now lapsed (or, I sometimes joke, post-vegetarian). The fries today are very, very salty and, I have to admit, tasty, in a chemical-laced sort of way. An enormous golden eagle being chased by a seagull flies toward the window and up and over the store. The hills and the Yukon River lie beyond the RVs in the parking lot.

———

The original inspiration for me to visit this particular Walmart came from the Whitehorse-born-and-raised writer and storyteller Ivan Coyote. I've been reading Coyote's rurally inflected trans sensibilities for many years, and I've seen them a few times now in performance (pronoun note: Coyote uses "they," though also criticizes our being so focused on the issue[13]). I have always appreciated Coyote's wry wit, vulnerable honesty and down-to-earth, hard-working sensibility. The contents of their writing are a far cry from the hip Montreal coffee shop where I sit and edit these words, and they would surely be able to offer an appropriately sarcastic observation about these too-cool holes in the wall. On the other hand, my soy latte arrived with a nice little leaf design in the foam, and was delicious.

Ivan Coyote describes life in the north in a lot of their work. In these pieces, the north comes off as a cold, hard, yet hospitable and friendly sort of place. The sort of place where those who come from outside will be tolerated and understood – even shown some of the ways of the northern bush – but will still be held at a bit of a distance. The north in Coyote's work is northern lights, the folly and heartiness of those who followed the Klondike gold rush, camp-outs in the bush, pickup trucks, beers, the complexity of lives lived in harsh circumstances, sprawling families both chosen and biological and the ability to laugh at one's own foibles.

In the 2008 book *The Slow Fix*, a collection of stories and performance pieces, Coyote turns their attention to the Walmart in Whitehorse. As is often the case in their writing, the actual subjects of the conversation – the Walmart and its effects – enter the conversation from the side, as part of a seeming digression. Coyote is, it seems at first, intent on describing Two Mile Hill, one of the two ways to drive down into the centre of town from the Alaska Highway. They begin by talking about what the experience of driving down the hill used to be like, when the hill bottomed out at a marsh. Coyote describes the wildlife springing from the bush around the marsh, ending with a wonderful description of a lynx gliding out of the bush and crossing the road "in four satiny strides."[14] The road curled under clay cliffs and brought one into town through the wetland, and the road refused to be renamed Jack London Boulevard, despite a government initiative to render the area both more metric – by getting rid of the reference to miles – and more tourist-friendly – by invoking one of the famous writers who have recorded the place in their work.

It is here, at the bottom of Two Mile Hill, that we encounter Coyote's description of Walmart. It is worth quoting at length. It can also be found online, recorded as part of the performance show *You Are Here* (which was also released on CD). Coyote, in the written version, states the following:

> A few years back, Wal-Mart talked the City of Whitehorse into paying several million taxpayer dollars to backfill the marsh with gravel so they could build a store there. Think of the jobs it will create, my aunties argued with me, think of the bargains, finally we won't have to pay whatever the shops on Main Street decide we're going to have to pay for a new pair of jeans, plus there will be a pharmacy and one of those machines you can print up your digital photos on, with the red-eye remover and the white borders and the whole nine yards, just like you see in the big malls down south. Finally, everything you can get in Vancouver or Edmonton, but without the plane ride.[15]

The debate is a familiar one, and the scenario is one that I've heard about at least anecdotally from Salmon Arm to Sylvan Lake and well beyond. The economics of saving a buck are, of course, very real, but it is the other costs that worry Coyote. They go on to say the following: "Now when you drive down the Two Mile Hill and take the corner that still wraps itself around the end of the clay cliffs, you pass the Wal-Mart, two car lots, a Radio Shack, a dollar store, a family restaurant, and a drive-thru Starbucks that all squat in a neon square bordered by a sidewalk where the marsh used to be. The gateway to the last frontier now looks a lot like Prince George, or Fort St. John or Thunder Bay or Red Deer."[16] The newly homogenized landscape is all but unrecognizable for Coyote, except for the few traces that remain of the place that used to be. The landscape has permanently changed and erased the Whitehorse in which they grew up.

That said, the traces that remain of the Whitehorse that Coyote recognizes and loves are important. You can find them if you look hard enough. "If it wasn't for the sideways sloping shadows that stretch across the chip seal under the midnight sun," Coyote writes, "if it wasn't for the wind-worn spine of the clay cliffs sheltering the place where the marsh used to be, if it wasn't for the shape of the curves in the river that still runs past where they built the Wal-Mart, maybe I wouldn't know I was home at all."[17] The scene is shot through with nostalgia, for a Whitehorse that exists only in the writer's mind, in the place where the mundane details of the quotidian can be stripped bare and in which the possibility of a cleaner, saner world can still exist. It is a place that only exists in the imaginary, and we can observe right away that, for instance, the particular curve of the riverbed in Whitehorse is itself a new one: today's swiftly eddying version of the river, the one that Coyote invokes, is one that has been subject to human interference before Walmart came along, in the form of the dam just upstream from town that has tamed the Whitehorse rapids and made the waters navigable for the kayaks and canoes that float along during our visit north. The lynx bounds across the road and out of sight; humankind has left its tracks rather more enduringly.

—

After pausing at the McDonald's, we head into Walmart's shoe section: later in the day we are going to a local hot springs that said on its website that we need to supply our own flip-flops. I also need to find my father a gift for Father's Day. We get up and wade through the crowd of white and Indigenous folks to see what we can find.

Flip-flops: four dollars for each pair. Father's Day gift: a Superman tank top that I buy for my dad partly in jest (he might think it's cool, who knows?). A large chocolate bar – today, they happen to be stocking pretty much every Dairy Milk flavour except for the fair trade one – two dollars. I have to admit it: everything here is extremely cheap, just as expected. We poke around and discuss class consciousness. A few years ago, I read a book called *The Age of Access*, by Jeremy Rifkin.[18] In it, Rifkin argues that, in the future, the affluent will no longer bother owning things, but will, instead, simply pay to access things when necessary. Doing so keeps capital mobile and makes it possible not to be so encumbered by ownership. Walmart, however, is the flip side to the age of access: everything here ties buyers into the ownership of things. Things that are, as one person I spoke with wryly put it, simply making a stop at Walmart on their way to the landfill. My partner and I speak about how people in North American suburbs negotiate their relationship to things, to ownership. We discuss our own, highly ambivalent, mobile and shifting relationships to class structures:

we are prone to making light of owning a Paris-themed towel or soap dispenser (as we see in the bath section). But we note both how sad and aspirational the soap dispenser is, too. It is there possibly to highlight an unrealized desire for travel for the consumer who buys it, or else to trigger a memory of the time in one's life when such travel was possible. That we have been to Paris, too, emphasizes our distance from this place, something that makes me profoundly uncomfortable as I put it here on the page (and leaves me wanting to protest, perhaps defensively, that our travels come in spite of my partner's working-class childhood and my parents having grown up in families with little money, on farms in the northern Alberta bush).

When we go to the checkout, we choose the most bored-looking checkout clerk, a young South Asian woman. We smile at her and she, for just a moment, flashes a smile in response before she turns to bagging up our things. We look at the "as seen on TV" impulse items and the celebrity magazines next to the till, then head back to McDonald's for lunch in order to complete the experience. We settle upon, of all strange things, a McLobster "sandwich" and more of those salty fries.

—

While I am planning this exploration of Walmart in White-horse, some friends point me in the direction of a researcher based at Thompson Rivers University in Kamloops, BC, named Lisa Cooke. While there is already a large amount of literature on Walmart in general, it also turns out that I'm really not the first person to have taken an interest in studying this particular Walmart location. Not too long after it was built, Cooke spent a great deal of time in the parking lot of the Whitehorse Walmart over three summers as part of her research for her doctoral dissertation. Her dissertation is an examination of the ways in which the ideas of the north and of the Yukon are created in the minds of travellers and locals. She very generously shared with me some of her unpublished work on the Walmart in Whitehorse, for which I remain grateful.

Cooke's dissertation has a whole fantastic chapter in which she records her experiences of interacting with people camped in RVs in the Walmart parking lot – exactly the same sorts of people who park their RVs here on our solstice visit to the store. What Cooke discovers is that, for many of these campers, while they may be somewhat ambivalent about the idea of camping out in front of a Walmart, they are nevertheless awestruck by the nature that they see on display in the north. They are awestruck even if it is a version of nature that is mediated by Walmart, like watching a bald eagle over the river from the vantage point of the parking lot – or witnessing the eagle that we saw from inside the McDonald's. Indeed, Cooke finds that folks tend to like their nature mediated, safe, on the other side of the windshield or glass, and preferably at some distance.

What I most appreciate about Cooke's approach is the generosity of spirit that she brings to her analysis. While she recognizes the many ways in which Walmart, as a corporation, can be critiqued – and she has done her homework on that score – she meets the people with whom she interacts with humility and openness. In fact, she realizes, the people who camp at Walmart aren't wrong when they feel like they are out in nature even when they are in their RVs on the asphalt. They *are* experiencing nature from the parking lot. They are even doing so with such sincerity that Cooke realizes that she is looking for irony where there may not be any. Nature, like other commodities, is in fact on sale at Walmart.[19] While we may want to view Walmart, as Coyote initially seems to, as a blight on the landscape and a source of profound discontent, the concept of nature is itself hardly unsullied. Nature is something that we might think of as being in opposition to culture, but both of these terms implicitly require humans to be there in order to determine which is which – meaning that both are part of human life, and hence part of culture. Nature is cultural, at least in that linguistic sense. At a minimum, we can see that both are markers of something – a divide – that is a bit ineffable when put under the microscope: the line between them shifts depending on our perspective.

Cooke discovers that the particular version of nature that Walmart campers wish to experience differs from her own understanding of what nature is. In the end, though, she grants that it is her own understanding of nature that is too restrictive. I find her take refreshing: Cooke's work signals that separating ourselves from the world of Walmart is indeed something that relies on our own values and judgments. While the corporation may be one against which we can position ourselves, the people who shop there do not deserve our scorn (as expressed, for instance, on the frankly cruel website peopleofwalmart.com). Instead, many of us are Walmart shoppers at one time or another; we're part of a continuum. I can now count myself among them. Most North Americans, after all, live very close to a Walmart and, when I was speaking with people in advance of writing this chapter, almost everyone I spoke with had visited a Walmart in the past, making me the odd one out.[20] In many places now, after all, especially semi-rural or suburban ones, Walmart exists as the local grocery store, pharmacy, hardware store, clothing store and more.

———

As we leave Walmart, it occurs to me – and not for the first time – that from a certain perspective I am a terrible person. Terrible in many of the ways that white, middle-class North Americans are terrible, consuming their way across the planet and leaving devastation in their wake. It is criticism that folks with privilege need, I think, to hear and accept. I aspire to be better, but fail in so many ways in spite of my sometimes very sustained efforts. Everyone I spoke with in preparation for this trip – those people who had all visited the store at least once – had a scathing analysis of Walmart. In writing this chapter, it was tempting for me to fall into the same analysis too, to separate myself from it. Yet I felt my continuity and complicity with the society that brings Walmart into being. So I tried different approaches. I tried, in some of my conversations, to offer a counter-analysis: Walmart is cheap for working-class folks; Walmart's just-in-time manufacturing model is actually very efficient; and Walmart will hire, for instance, newcomers who might otherwise not be considered by other employers. Yes, there are very good counter-arguments to each of those statements. But I am nevertheless at Walmart as a class tourist. I can't let myself be haughty or superior, because that would simply be a way to reproduce and extend my own privileges.

When I look around the store, I see a far greater diversity of people than I do in the corridors of the university in which I work. Many class backgrounds, cultural backgrounds, abilities, ages, sexualities and genders are visible in Walmart. Many people are enjoying themselves. The kids with the Happy Meals are happy. The shoppers are able to keep themselves and their families fed and clothed until the next paycheque. I am free to walk back into the sunshine and shop at organic markets and fair trade clothing stores to my heart's content. All of which makes me wonder whose interests my boycott has really served. As we leave, we see that many more RVs have pulled into the parking lot.

—

The next time that Ivan Coyote brings up the Walmart in *The Slow Fix* is toward the end of the book. They have just been in another store, one in downtown Whitehorse, buying a map of permafrost regions of Canada and talking with the disinterested checkout clerk. In the process, Coyote shares a bit of knowledge about permafrost, and about how the buildings in Whitehorse shifted and buckled until building codes were updated to account for the frozen ground. Even with the climate accounted for, though, Whitehorse cannot support any tall structures. This knowledge leads Coyote to consider what happens as the ground warms due to climate change, something that is an acute problem at extreme northern and southern latitudes, where average temperatures are rising more than elsewhere in the world.[21] "What would happen," Coyote wonders, "if the permafrost all melts? The Wal-Mart was bad enough. What would stop them from building twelve-storey condominium towers right downtown with a comfortable view of the river?"[22] Curiously enough, Walmart here becomes the bringer of its own unique brand of gentrification, of southern-style (which in this context means Vancouver-style) urban living. The Walmart and the thawing ground are also indicators of the same trend: humans clambering across the Earth in search of bargains, of novelty and of a place to practice the individualism that is a hallmark of both consumer culture and Western liberalism.

The Walmart in Whitehorse appears one last time, on the second last page of the book, when Coyote realizes that, in spite of it all, many things do not change. Coyote writes:

My last trip home, I realized that even Wal-Mart and permafrost-proof skyscrapers and global warming will never make the sun go down any earlier in the month of June in my hometown, and that thirty below is still thirty below, no matter how close you get to park your truck to the front door of the mall. A three-in-the-morning sun will still cast sideways shadows every summer, and the slow curve of the clay cliffs will always cut the cold wind in half as soon as you round the corner halfway down the road we never stopped calling the Two Mile Hill.[23]

Walmart, in other words, does damage to the land, and to the spirit of Whitehorse and to the north, but it can only do so much damage. The weather and its overall patterns will remain. The Earth continues to orbit the sun, leading to the warm midnights of summer solstices in the far north, as well as the deep chill of mid-winter. Walmart has, of course, taken on a metaphorical resonance in Coyote's book, too. It is a symbol for the destruction of nature, a symbol for the south, for capitalism and consumerism and for human sloth. It is a symbol for many things that could be summarized as "not good," in other words. It is a perpetual menace that I can imagine Coyote shaking a fist at every time that they drive down Two Mile Hill in an old half-ton pickup truck. And yet, for all of that, the Walmart in Whitehorse is something that has destroyed neither the town nor its spirit. The spirit will go on: there are bigger forces at work.

—

During the remainder of our brief time in the Yukon, we take in other sights. They are putting up condominium buildings with a good view of the river, but the condos are only maybe six storeys or so. Solstice is a good time to be there: it doesn't really get dark, though the sun does go down briefly, and folks are in good spirits. For solstice night, Whitehorse has organized a Nuit Blanche arts festival, which we attend. The highlight comes at around one a.m., when we discover an interactive sound installation in the trolley house down by the river and join others using railway spikes to play piano strings that have been attached to railway ties and linked into amplifiers. The effect is rhythmic and curiously communal: the taut strings, one per player, thrum a low, tonal beat that we improvise together across the wide room. Later, after walking around downtown some more, we see musicians playing over on a stretch of ground once called Whiskey Flats and watch some performance art in front of a bookstore.

The next day, Sunday, is National Aboriginal Day. We head to the very welcoming Kwanlin Dün Cultural Centre, where local Indigenous and non-Indigenous folks come together for the day. There are dancers and music and vendors and food and many, many people in attendance. It is an optimistic time, though the feeling is partly undercut later on when, while walking around the town, an Indigenous man from up in the far north pulls us aside to tell us about how most of his friends have died by suicide. We talk to him for a while next to the old log church and thank him for his time.

We wrap up our trip with a tour of the local brewery and with a trail ride on the morning of our flight. I feel like I have learned quite a bit during this short trip. It feels like an introduction to something more sustained, a relationship to the north to be continued at a later date. I lament that I am unable to travel farther up north for this project, to see smaller communities that are governed, at some level, by what's available at the local Northern Store.

Everywhere that we go in Whitehorse, folks are friendly and talkative. They are, typically, curious about what it is that has brought us north. My answer – Walmart and this book – tends to elicit a reaction of surprise. That their Walmart has already been studied and written about also comes as a surprise. That such a thing might bring one north is not the usual story of trekking the Alaska or Klondike highways. Many folks express interest in the topic of the book, but, in general, it seems that locals do not wish to be summed up by their Walmart. And so I discover that I need to expand my lens beyond the southern arrogance and hubris that first brought me here. Luckily, Yukoners appear to be generous of heart and seem to allow for folks from elsewhere to be naive about the place, provided that they are willing to learn.

On the morning of the trail ride, our guide pauses on a ridge near Fox Lake, just north of Lake Laberge, which I first heard of in the poems of Robert Service. Our horses eat as much of the grasses as they can while we are stopped. We are looking across to a mountain range that I do not know. There are no other people in sight. "Look," my partner says at one point. Overhead, a hawk flies, screeching down as if to remind us that we are not from there, that we do not know what we are doing there – and to remind us that, like the Walmart and all of consumer culture, we are just passing through.

Cracks in the Concrete:
Kitsilano and Beyond

It's a Sunday in late June, and I am sitting in an ice cream shop on West 4th Avenue in Vancouver. At a couple of blocks west of Burrard Street, I'm in the heart of Kitsilano, a neighbourhood that we might equate with yoga and affluence, even though the overwhelming majority of Kits residents are renters and only the extremely wealthy can afford real estate in Vancouver these days.[1] Vancouverites seem to love to talk about the price of real estate, as though it were a morbid fascination. As I write, the issue is coming to a boil once again and everyone is watching to see what will happen. West 4th is a mix of marijuana shops ("clubs" in the parlance of the moment), clothing shops, sushi restaurants and yoga studios. I can see all of these and more from where I am sitting.

If you have the sense by now that I spend a lot of time in different places around Canada, I share that feeling; I maintain relations of both blood family and chosen kin in many places in this country, and feel like I'm often on the move. I am in Vancouver for my sister's wedding, which happened yesterday, and the guests have now dispersed. Earlier this morning, we met up with two dear friends and their toddler at the Granville Island playground and splash park. When I was young, I played in the same playground, with its signature yellow waterslide, and today I watched as my daughter went down the slide, far more daring than I was at her age. (She may be more daring than I am now, even: she – at the age of seven – talked me into taking my first ride on a roller coaster that went all the way upside down. It was exciting, even if it wasn't the Mindbender at West Edmonton Mall.)

Granville Island is a lovely phenomenon, if not unproblematic. It is a curious mix of art studios, Emily Carr University of Art + Design, a concrete factory, the children's market, shops and the food market. Underneath the Granville Street Bridge and situated on False Creek, it is at once urban and marine. Its shops are expensive, certainly, and absolutely aimed at visitors to Vancouver – although some Vancouverites shop here too, especially in the farmer's market. Even the seagulls know, though, that many of the visitors are from out of town: they stake out an awning above one of the doors that lets out from the back of the market to the waterfront. They watch for people carrying precariously balanced plates of lunch to the outdoor benches. Out-of-towners love to sit outside and catch the view: those seats overlook the water that stretches toward English Bay and out to the Salish Sea and the Pacific Ocean beyond. When an unsuspecting tourist exits the market, the lead bird swoops in, deliberately knocking the food to the ground if possible. At this point, all of the other birds descend and feast. The unsuspecting tourist's lunch is gone within moments. I've seen it happen several times on different visits and have myself been the target of just such an ambush. It is pattern enough not to be chance, whatever we might say about avian behaviour. I can't begrudge the birds, either: it's a spot with plentiful good eats and lots of rubes who keep on providing the grub. It seems to me that fish and chips are the birds' favourite dish. Nearby, Granville Island maintains other services that cater to local Vancouverites, with a community centre that runs a kayak and canoe club. This area is well integrated into the fabric of middle-class Vancouver life.[2]

———

In his 2011 book of poetry entitled *Mannequin Rising*, poet, critic and activist Roy Miki includes a long poem called "A Walk on Granville Island." Miki, whose work I've read for a long time now, is today a retired faculty member from Simon Fraser University. He was born in Manitoba, to parents who were displaced as a result of the internment measures taken by the Canadian government against people of Japanese descent during the Second World War. Miki was highly involved in the Redress Movement that sought reparations from the Canadian government, and he is an important member of Canadian literary communities, someone who always pushes his experimental practice to its limits. *Mannequin Rising*, Miki's sixth book of poetry, is an interrogation of the cultures of late capitalism, a book that roves from Vancouver to Japan and back again, integrating photo collages of the interactions of commercial spaces with natural elements like pigeons and plant life. Throughout the book, the figure of the mannequin shows up, silently posing questions to readers about how we interact with the flashing lights of globality. Sometimes the mannequins are us, faceless and consuming, while other times they watch our quizzical behaviour from a position of remove.

"A Walk on Granville Island" opens with those pesky Granville Island gulls, as follows:

Today the rambunctious gulls (above)
squawk about the resurrection of sky
lines / the hallowed out angles that
festoon our gregarious sentiments

The social but paranoid crows (below)
discourse on the lowly virtue of hand
picked local produce / feigning the
trendy bundle of cross purposes.[3]

The birds stand in for some of the positions that Vancouverites might occupy: the gulls squawking over sightlines might represent one of the ongoing concerns of real estate developers in the city, as it is a city in which a good sightline – a view of the water or of the mountains – can be worth a few million bucks' worth of "gregarious sentiment." The paranoid crows, in turn, may mark some of the city's other local sentiments, the sorts of greenscape thinking captured in projects like the well-known book *The 100-Mile Diet*, by Alisa Smith and J.B. MacKinnon.[4] Hand-picked local produce is virtuous, and ideally humbly so.

But what of those "cross purposes"? Vancouver, and consumption in Vancouver, does indeed often seem to be at cross purposes: How can everyone get to enjoy (or consume) a nice sightline when space is finite? After all, for one person to be able to enjoy a fine sightline through the matrix of private property ownership means that someone else is deprived of it. How, at the same time, can Vancouverites come together to extoll communally grown local produce? How can one be virtuous, consuming less, while also buying a new yoga mat? "It could be that a walk / along the seawall arrests / the detached thought," Miki supposes.[5] Vancouver can be a sea of contradictions, as we see when consumers and shoppers meander through Miki's poetry: even if it's a contradiction in terms, in the city people do things like "bottle entropy / as a brand to die for."[6] Pigeons and starlings occupy urban spaces and fly around Granville Island, while the historical voyage of George Vancouver in 1792 into False Creek haunts the city, his name a reminder of the colonization of the land.

It is in this space that the figure of the mannequin enters, standing in contrast to the humans who shop at Granville Island. As the day described in the poem wears on, Miki's verse comes to echo T.S. Eliot:

> Let us go then you and you and you
> before the market closes all we have
> are the track suits on our backs each
> gut wrenching outfit record for
> posterity on our minds bent to wards
>
> Organic silences weigh in at double
> the rate of those inflected with pesticidal
> harmonic brand through subtle alternatives
>
> Mannequins need to consider delicacy
> in these fades of fission friendly (FFF)
> when to hold shape is utterly composure.[7]

As opposed to shoppers like Miki, festooned merely with unappealing, gut-wrenching track suits, the mannequins stand there, impassive. The shoppers' bodies come off as frenetic, unfashionable, assembling bits and pieces of consumer culture into an uncomfortable whole. The mannequins, on the other hand, are different figures: they are granted a stillness in the middle of consumerism; they get to "consider" things, like the fading materials around them; they get to retain their "composure" and hold their shape. As such, the walk through Granville Island is one of contrasts: the birds stand in for different positions that humans may take, the long history of colonization haunts the space and the humans bustle through in their dishevelled outfits while the mannequins are able to quietly remain. They are the sentries who contemplate the market.

—

After we leave Granville Island, we head toward Kitsilano via West 1st Avenue, passing, first, the Lamborghini, Bentley and Jaguar dealerships, then the "Welcome to Kitsilano" sign when we jump down to Cornwall Avenue. The sign is immediately opposite the head office of lululemon, the by-now iconic marker of Vancouver's singular contribution to global athletics: yoga wear. The head office, on Burrard and Cornwall, is an older brown brick building. We park on a side street, and my partner and our kids send me off for a couple of hours' exploration and writing before we meet up again in the ice cream shop. Now, they are merrily enjoying three ice creams that added up to twenty dollars. Is the twenty-dollar bill the Kitsilano loonie? Behind me, I overhear young Vancouver hipsters who are discussing the relative merits of Tokyo and Paris, and who are talking about selling things on Etsy.

We leave the ice cream shop and walk up West 4th, and then stop again outside the 49th Parallel coffee shop at Yew, a place that I came to once before with my sister. The sky has clouded over, and we get a few drips of late afternoon drizzle. The weather has turned distinctly Vancouver-ish. As we walk along, luxury cars drive past. Range Rovers are popular today, and so are Porsches. At the same time, homeless folks are visible on street corners. We are a long way from the Downtown Eastside here, a place often known as Canada's poorest postal code, and a neighbourhood that is a far cry from the seeming affluence – the conspicuous consumption – of many Vancouverites.[8]

Before we stopped to sit, we lingered over a store called Ayoub's Dried Fruits & Nuts, a remarkably beautiful shop in which each of the displays sat in a large pewter dish under elaborate chandeliers, all of which evoked a bygone Baroque sensibility. It was lavish and excessive, and again a sharp contrast to the homelessness in the city. I learn later that Ayoub's has five locations, no less. I think of the episode of the satirical show *Portlandia* in which two characters find themselves in an artisanal knot store run by guest star Jeff Goldblum, who plays the character Alan. The couple is looking for a housewarming gift for a friend and have read about the supposed trend of artisanal knots in the Sunday *Times*. They eventually settle on an artisanal knot made out of iPhone earbuds and set under glass, a gift that Alan extols as being tasteful and trendy. But then the punchline arrives when they get to the party and everyone else has brought exactly the same gift. The improbability of a store devoted to selling knotted bits of rope was about equal to the curatorial delight and excess of Ayoub's. And yet, such stores can and do thrive under the right conditions.

———

The other long poem in Roy Miki's *Mannequin Rising* is set in Kitsilano, and is titled "Scoping (also pronounced Shopping) in Kits." The title is worth parsing, because it very usefully suggests something that connects to my overall purpose with this book. Miki suggests that the words "scoping" and "shopping" can, at a minimum, be pronounced in the same way. Shopping is common enough; I've been on that theme throughout. But scoping? In the first instance, it is the participle of the verb "to scope." But a section early in Miki's poem suggests that he has something else in mind, when he writes that "The scop in shopping / tumbles off the tongue."[9] To me, that gets interesting (if a bit difficult to decipher; Miki's poetry always takes a bit of – very worthwhile – work). What is a scop? In Old English, a scop is a poet, someone who makes or recites poetry. Etymologically, the word relates to the verb "scapan," from which we get the verb "to shape" in modern English. So, as given in Old English, to be a poet is to be a shaper of language: the poet shapes or, even, the shaper shapes. What Miki suggests then is that to be a poet is similar to being a shopper when he tells us that "scoping" and "shopping" sound the same. I'm yet to find evidence that "shopping" and "scoping" share etymological roots – shopping has a different path through Germanic languages, and seems to be more linked to the physical buildings in which things are sold (shops, that is). Nevertheless, to extend Miki's title for the poem, the shaper of language and the buyer of goods are similar. How so? Both are involved in processes of shaping life, but I'm interested in digging further.

Throughout the poem on Kitsilano, we see the poet interacting with commercial spaces. The "poet survives / across zones in market / conditions" and charts a path through the culture of late capitalism. He watches the mannequins, which, he suggests, "must share / foreknowledge of the rise / and fall of human desires." In this environment, and in a tone of seeming exasperation, the speaker states that "We are consumers get used to it / if we are here because you were / there and there is always a here."[10] Put differently, we are all consumers within a globalizing marketplace in which sameness is often enforced across great distances; the poet is not separate from this world. In fact, the poet is an active participant in this world, shaping it through language just as commerce shapes it through sale. In a later piece on lululemon (and the "scandal" of their seaweed-based clothing not containing any actual seaweed[11]), Miki goes on to wonder just how enmeshed in this world we all may be:

> Is a commodity
> a companion
>
> Is a patent
> a belonger
>
> Is a brand
> a friend
> …
> Is a store
> a commune
>
> Is a window
> a scribe
>
> Is a frame
> a blame
>
> Is a choice
> a ruse[?][12]

This series of statements, phrased as questions but without the expected punctuation, needs interrogation. When we wonder whether a commodity might be a companion, just as whether a brand might be a friend, we are asking not only about brand loyalty but also about the feelings that we attach to inanimate objects. How do we make friends or companions out of the goods that we buy? I think right away of the anxiety that many people feel when they do not have their mobile devices on hand, or the way that we rely on a particular pair of shoes to get us through the day. We do indeed maintain the companionship of the items that we buy. Does this situation in turn mean that a store on West 4th Avenue is a commune? Some storefronts might establish themselves as co-operatives or as communal spaces (or, say, medicinal clubs), but is it the same thing? While Miki's questions initially seem absurd, they are, after I give them more thought, useful provocations. Is, for instance, a window a scribe? Here, once again, the shop and the poet bump into each other. There is a history to window dressing, to dioramas and to commercial photography – a history that suggests that the window was, especially in the early twentieth century, considered to be an art form, thus approaching the work of the poet.[13] In that sense, a display window can perform the work of a scribe, shaping the desirability of objects displayed to potential consumers.

In the end, though, Miki asks: Is the choice that we are given, the choice, say, of products, simply a "ruse"? Are we seemingly presented with choices as we window-shop through Kitsilano, only to realize that every time that we make a choice we are making no choice at all, because each consumer decision only reinforces the fact that we are consumers deciding from a predetermined set of variables? On the one hand, surely this is the case; on the other hand, Miki does not answer the question and leaves it hanging. What does it mean, too, if the window is a scribe – or rather, if the scribe's work, the work of the scop, is somehow also the work of shopping? The implication is that the poet is part of the marketplace and part of the ruse. Whether that poet is a contented one or a rebellious dissident, she or he is nevertheless a part of this world. If scoping and shopping are one and the same, then we have to recognize the ways in which poets are commodified – their books exist in relation to the market against which so much art rails. As Miki records the mannequins of Kitsilano then, he recognizes that living and writing in late capitalism are related things, and he sees complicity between the humans on the streets and the shops all around.

—

When I walk around Vancouver, I am often struck by the concrete in the city: the particular mix that went into many of the sidewalks – those of a certain vintage – has a different texture than that of any other city of which I am aware. It is pebbled and dark grey; in its cracks, mosses and small plants push their way up. Even if the human species is destroying the environment at such a rate that we can and should expect a massive die-off of species over the next generations, I am nevertheless impressed by the robust networks of roots that push back against the concrete in Vancouver streets. The Pacific Ocean – which you can see, even dip your toes into, from parts of Kits – is clogging up with plastic: the Great Pacific Garbage Patch, an area roughly twice the size of Texas, is a morass of micro-plastics that are moving into the food chain; the forests in BC and around the world are still being sawed down at alarming rates.[14] Plant life, however, fights back. I think, for instance, of the poet Lisa Robertson's writing on the Himalayan blackberry in Vancouver.[15] The blackberry is an invasive yet tasty species that grows in the back alleys of Kitsilano at an incredible rate, taking over underused spaces. The berries feed the birds and the bugs, and are one of the first plant species to take over spaces that humans have vacated. As an invasive species, blackberries may pose problems, but they are a ubiquitous and scrumptious reminder of the tenuous hold that humans maintain over the spaces that we have temporarily declared to be ours.

Vancouver is constantly changing in other ways, too. For years, one of the most notorious commercial oddities of the city was the Starbucks corner at Robson and Thurlow, where two locations of the Seattle-based coffee chain competed against each other on opposite corners of the intersection. The situation was mocked for being ridiculous, and Vancouverites' addiction to the caffeinated green mermaid were satirized. Yet, the twin locations made perfect sense because of the volume of coffee drinkers, and also received, through mockery, a sort of ironically positive press. One of the two locations recently closed up when their lease ran out, and so there is now only one place to get a Venti Americano at Robson and Thurlow; but as ever, the shift reminds me of how temporary and transitory these spaces are. That corner puts me in mind of the novel *Stanley Park* by Timothy Taylor, a novel that, structurally, pits the possibilities of anarchic living based on sustenance scavenging in Vancouver's massive Stanley Park against the haute cuisine of the ever-shifting menus of wealthy restauranteurs.[16] Leases expire, restaurants and other stores change, and the city is always in a form of human motion that is only temporarily, if ever, removed from the changes wrought by the natural world.

Should we lament these ongoing human changes? This question, I suppose, is one that vexes me most when I think about

Vancouver as a whole, from when I lived in the city as a young kid right up to the present. It's not dissimilar to the question of whether to lament the disappearance of the Mom-and-Pop shops in small towns when Walmart moves in, as I discussed in the previous chapter. Vancouver's landscape has changed a great deal over time, from the small corner groceries of the mid-twentieth century that someone like Michael Kluckner documents in his nostalgic book *Vanishing Vancouver*, to the glass-and-nature global city that Douglas Coupland both celebrates and mocks in his book *City of Glass*.[17] While I prefer small shops to mall kiosks, and I prefer mall kiosks to shopping at Walmart, part of me sees precisely how small corner stores lead us toward Walmart in the long run. All are, in the end, part of the grand package of human consumption that leads us to the Great Pacific Garbage Patch. Some days I feel like we might be best served by amplifying the contradictions as much as possible so that we can see the problems in our world for what they are – and then shut it all down (there is a movement, "accelerationism," that builds on that line of thought). I can't really wish the problems to get worse, though. So on other days I am more compromising and recognize that changing capitalism – along with other societal ills such as white supremacy, sexism, homophobia and ableism – is a more complicated task. Those are the days when I feel like I can almost see the blackberry vines growing, slowly reclaiming the soil – or when I can hear the quiet dripping of the long-vanished waterways buried underneath Vancouver's streets, which lie dormant for the moment only.[18]

The fuller story of Vancouver pulls us out of the manicured environments of Granville Island and Kitsilano (and Kerrisdale and Point Grey and so on): the Greater Vancouver area is a tangle of suburbs and exurbs known in part for not having been built up with freeways in the manner of many North American cities in the second half of the twentieth century. Vancouver is often a snarl of traffic that slowly moves along corridors like Kingsway, a road that runs from Vancouver proper, branching off Main Street and then running southeast through Burnaby to its end in New Westminster. From my point of view, Kingsway is a more or less unremarkable road that runs from the Kingsgate Mall to Metrotown. From there, one ends up in what locals term the Lower Mainland, a semi-rural, semi-suburban spread that goes all the way to Hope, where the Fraser River enters the valley. It is beautiful, but also a place riddled with contradictions and social ills (sort of like anywhere, though with its own local challenges); I view it as a very mixed place.

Michael Turner, in his 1995 book of poetry *Kingsway*, characterizes the road and the area around it as a depressing, rundown urban environment. In a prose poem in the collection, he writes the following comparison to Burnaby's Metrotown: "Look what happened at Kingsgate Mall. You can tell where they're at by the decline in their Santa Clauses. An Eaton's instead of a Saan. And we've got a SkyTrain stop. Like, my friends down at VLC Properties. Like, just the other day. I don't wear a suit for nothing, you know."[19] The piece has the tone of an overheard phone conversation, with only one half being recorded for the reader. The conversation's anxiety appears to be that Metrotown could worsen just like Kingsgate, a mall that Turner depicts as being in a dreadful state of decline.

All along Turner's Kingsway, dodgy things happen in parking lots, violence is just around the corner and poverty is perpetual. It is the sort of commercial strip on which falling apart, decrepit signage advertises yesteryear's novelties, as in the poem "The Idea of a Street":

EVERYTHING MUST GO
so you go
NEXT YEAR'S MODELS IN NOW
so you drive by
and like the red one
it makes you hungry
so you DRIVE THRU
to the line up
TRY OUR BACON DOUBLE-CHEESE
so you try one
'cause you're like that.[20]

This bland environment of being told what to do brings down the "you" of this poem, the you who gets a bacon double cheeseburger at the drive-thru window on the way to the next store, the next sale, the next bargain. The misspelled signs are simply part of the kitsch, the allure of a place that may view itself as being outside of culture, outside of the interest of something like a poem. Its lack of self-consciousness, in its own way, becomes poetic. As the spaces of commerce are encoded into the poetic line, we see that they become cultural. Or, rather, we see the ways in which they always already were cultural: the spaces of the everyday are, or rather create, the cultures within which we live.

—

Across the Lower Mainland, the question of how to live is constant, in a place that is bordered to the south by the United States, to the west by the Pacific Ocean, and to the east and north by the Rocky Mountains. Housing has been progressively creeping up the slopes of the North Shore for a long time now; I can see the spread from many angles while walking in the city. An often-derided suburb like Surrey has been densifying, and people are likely now – as they have been for some time – to claim to be from or close to South Surrey in order to avoid the stigma of the rougher bits of that municipal division (the rougher bits being those from whence, in part, my partner's family comes). In Richmond, where I lived for some years when I was young, there have recently been debates about whether legislation should be enacted to require that English be placed on signs alongside the customary Chinese (in a debate that strikes me, at least from a distance, as being reminiscent of language law debates in Quebec).[21] When I travel around the city, I feel that Vancouver is indeed very distinct from the rest of Canada. There is an ethos that I might too hastily describe as one of libertarian individualism, visible in many places: Vancouver is highly eco-conscious, and well-tanned middle-class Vancouverites (many of them white) enjoy the outdoors and playing volleyball on the beaches in Kitsilano and English Bay. At the same time, not far away, individuals are left to fend for themselves in the Downtown Eastside, or, even within the working middle class, struggle to find adequate housing in a desperately expensive environment (with "foreign" – read "racialized" – money often blamed as the root of the evil, something that is not without its own vexed complexities). Vancouver seems rife with contradictions – many of which Vancouverites are at work themselves to challenge. Lotusland has become a place of some discontent, much of it based upon disagreements about how to use – or consume – the unceded Musqueam, Squamish and Tsleil-Waututh Indigenous lands upon which the city is built.

—

In the final piece in *Kingsway*, Turner suggests that "you" had

> ...better buy
> stuff at the retail price so
> the corner store can continue
> and lease a new car every year
> so you'll never have to
> get it tested then
> stop driving.[22]

The first part of the statement demonstrates, in a sense, my previous point that all roads lead to Walmart: paying for stuff at retail price might keep the corner store in business, but it is not the most economical way to shop. The statement inhabits its own sense of nostalgia by slyly acknowledging that we are unlikely to keep paying the retail price for things when we don't have to. This culture of convenience is summed up in the newly leased car every year that prevents "you" from having to think about inconvenient things, like maintenance. However, in the end, we will all stop driving: we will consume for a while, and then die. Life on the Kingsway, life in the suburbs, is, in this sense, depressingly cyclical.

This cyclical life is also one that Douglas Coupland depicts with a great deal of cynical humour in his satirical 2007 novel *The Gum Thief*.[23] The novel is set in a Staples office supply store in the middle of suburbia, somewhere in the Lower Mainland. It stars Roger – a middle-aged, divorced alcoholic – and Bethany – a young woman emerging from a Goth phase – who both work at Staples. Within the novel, a second, nested novel, *Glove Pond*, emerges – a novel that Roger is in the midst of writing. The store is, in this book, a site of failure: to be consigned to working at "das Schtoop," as the book puts it, means that you weren't qualified for anything meaningful, at least in terms of how "meaning" has been understood. The oddball assortment of people who work in the store are the symbolic detritus of late capitalist culture and their immature, bullying behaviour is precisely the sort "race to the bottom" that may well be typical of trickle-down economics. To work at Staples, Coupland suggests, is to be at the bottom of the socio-economic food chain. Working in retail is a form of hell, or at least of incarceration: work, eat, sleep, repeat. The goal is to pay the rent so as to be able to continue to go to work so as to be able to continue to pay the rent.

And yet, the novel-within-the-novel, *Glove Pond*, turns the book on its head. *Glove Pond* shows that capitalist culture fails us at the "upper" registers, too. It's not just the denizens of Staples who are the dupes. *Glove Pond* stars Steve and Gloria, two run-down middle-aged bourgeois failures (one a professor, the other an actor), and Kyle and Brittany, two young rising stars (one a high-flying writer, the other a neurosurgeon). The sign of Kyle Falconcrest's success is the fifteen million dollar contract that he has just secured for his books (something that is about as rare as a unicorn's feather), while Gloria and Steve's failure is shown through their bad shopping habits: their old furniture and their lack of food betray the fact that they are horrible hosts, and horrible people, too. Even if caused by undisclosed trauma, their failure is marked by their particular failure as consumers. Their inability to host appropriately is marked, in particular, by the "be-weeviled" pancake mix that makes up the sum total of the food in the house. Kyle's success, in turn, is marked by the commercial viability of his works and his being young, being the next thing, rather than because his work has any intrinsic quality or merit.

As it comes together, we see that the novel-within-the-novel is a satire of social manners and norms – and so is *The Gum Thief* itself. Steve and Gloria's hosting collapses and the evening is a failure that leads to Brittany leaving Kyle. Now they too will become subject to the vicissitudes of life, their successes based upon their outward appearances and their failures deeply lodged in their hearts. As we step back from *Glove Pond*, the hero of the novel ends up, undoubtedly, being Roger. He and Bethany's mother, DeeDee, we imagine, are likely to spark a romantic connection, and he will rebuild his life because he is able to admit to his faults and revel, if not wallow, in them. Bethany is still in the middle of being formed and she will likely be okay, too, in spite of a suicide attempt. But, even more broadly speaking, the message of the novel is that the elites are corrupt, the bottom-feeders are dupes to capital and the customers are all jerks. At the same time, however, the only possibilities for cultural engagement are, it turns out, those that occur in places like Staples. Roger, we learn, embodies the only possible success: his novel is the only realistic form of non-corrupt art that can respond to late capitalist culture. Screw being at the middle of cultural life, Coupland suggests – in the middle of world cities like the Paris that Bethany visits and hates. That rat race, embodied by Steve, Gloria, Kyle and Brittany in *Glove Pond*, is just as hollow and corrupt as climbing the corporate ladder. Instead, art comes from those places like Staples that we shouldn't care about, but that are, nevertheless, exactly where we spend most of our time.

—

Late in *Mannequin Rising*, in a piece called "Viral Travels to Tokyo,"
Roy Miki writes the following stanza:

> In this surge of hybrid coalescence our bodies are
> conducive to being human or not. Viral as infrastructure
> finds voice in molecular networks in forms of 'social
> distancing.' Instead of shaking hands let's bump elbows
> and forget hugs and kisses. That's so pre-H1N1. Physical
> contact of any kind is so socially passé.[24]

While on the one hand the passage appears to be very tongue-
in-cheek, on the other hand it notes the ways in which turbo-
capitalism is also a mechanism of distancing us from one
another. Our hybrid coalescence with our devices – our Fitbits
and iPhones are the most obvious items today (sure soon to be
displaced by the newest thing), but so too are medical devices
like glasses, prostheses and pacemakers – render us, according to
some, "posthuman." For instance, the social distancing of social
media involves maintaining physical space between us. In this
milieu, Miki suggests, physical contact is "passé." This distancing
seems to be a consequence of the world in which we now live, a
consequence of a culture that is generated by surveillance, policing and infectious disease scares all around us. At the same time,
however, humans need physical contact in order to survive and
thrive. Vancouver, as a city of zones of consumption, from Granville Island and Kitsilano to the Downtown Eastside, to the malls
out in the suburbs and the shops on Kingsway, does a great deal
to separate bodies from one another, to compartmentalize them.
How do we bring nourishing, healthful physical contact back into

our exchanges? Perhaps it comes through learning to valorize, precisely, the ways in which culture happens at the edges, when we're not looking, in the places that we've long since been taught not to take seriously.

—

It's with all of this in mind that, some months later, we all go to Québec City to see Carnaval. When told that we would have the opportunity to live in Montreal for a year, my younger daughter said that the number one thing that she would like to do was to go and meet Bonhomme (Bonhomme's existence being, perhaps, the one standard of French immersion education all across Canada). Carnaval was a fantastically good time, and we spent our time also roaming the old city, discovering for ourselves where Samuel de Champlain lived, and so on. Quebec is a neat town, although we didn't get to see all that much of it, and getting to stay in the Château Frontenac was also a cool thing. The cheapest rooms were on sale – we stayed right next to the elevator. It was a first time for all of us to stay in a Fairmont hotel; we did our best not to look like we had just snuck in the back door so that we could warm our hands over the radiators.

Carnaval was the first place in a while where I saw selfie sticks in use. It was odd. People were walking around in the crowd, sticks extended, either photographing or recording themselves – often while downing their canes full of caribou. For the uninitiated, caribou is an alcohol-rich drink, served hot, that is just about perfect for stumbling around in bone-chilling temperatures. We sampled some between bouts of sledding down ice tracks and riding in dogsleds. People on the Carnaval rides were, similarly, recording the event on their phones or cameras.

For all of my engagements with consumer culture, I just don't understand selfie sticks. Why is it that we are so interested in producing our lives as spectacles in this manner? What is the selfie stick's endgame? Part of me anticipates that the end result is just more fully commodified bodies: our bodies themselves are becoming the products that we are producing for contemporary consumption. As in Vancouver, consumer culture risks compartmentalizing us more and more. There seems to be a veritable frenzy to become the most consumed body through social media. So the goal is to be consumed? By whom? To what end? The effects of this shift strike me as worrying, if not downright toxic, but asking the question of logical ends may be to miss the point. Where does our personal pleasure end and that of our viewers begin? People say that being "liked" or "hearted" on social media has serious psychological effects on us. In this context, can we enjoy the ride? Or is it just a brilliantly festooned track that takes us straight into some sort of murky underworld? I have no idea, but I fear that, for many, it is no longer possible to separate our pleasure from that of those who view our pleasure. Perhaps that means that we're all in it together, and maybe that's a good thing. Alternatively, maybe it means that we are turning over the control of our own pleasure, placing it into the hands of everyone else.

Either way, for now, I'll take a pass on the selfie stick. At Carnaval, I found it much better to watch the people in the giant hamster balls attempting to stay upright as they rolled down the snow-covered hillside in the Plains of Abraham than it would have been to try to record the mayhem. As with the waterslide at Granville Island, I enjoyed the rides that my daughters opted for and sipped on caribou, and noticed just how strange contemporary culture is when it's remixed by the dictates of late capitalism.

Bigger is Bigger:
West Edmonton Mall

For the sake of this project, I would like to go back to the malls of my childhood, because they have all changed. I misremember much of what they were like, I think. When I speak with people about malls, I encounter a remarkable amount of nostalgia, which I see also in a lot of the art, film and literature produced in or about malls. What makes us feel nostalgic for the malls of our childhoods? Nostalgia is messy at best. Perhaps you might not feel nostalgia, or you might resist it, feeling, as I used to, that malls are not the sorts of places about which one should feel any real sentimentality. But I've grown to look at it this way, at least as far as this book is concerned: I feel confident that anyone who reads *Malled* will feel dissatisfied with at least some portion of it, perhaps feeling that some bit of their own mall history should have been included. Have you noticed that I left out your favourite mall, or your childhood hangout, or some significant piece of consumer culture from your point of view? Do you mind? Why? When I spoke with people about this project, they almost invariably offered up their own local wisdom about malls in Hamilton or Saskatoon, or about what shopping in Corner Brook or

Yellowknife is like. I expect that you will feel that I haven't managed some aspect of this topic as well as I should have. People are often proud of their malls and shops, be they early malls, large malls or even unremarkable malls: they are places with which we became intimately familiar, down to the crumbling concrete that perhaps we once kicked with high-top sneakers, waiting for our parents to gather the clothes from the dry cleaners, or for groceries from the Safeway pickup lane. If that intimacy doesn't provide at least some form of grudging nostalgia then, reader, I salute you and am a tiny bit surprised.

When I think of the malls of my own childhood, West Edmonton Mall sticks out. It's the biggest mall in Canada still, if no longer the world. It's the alpha and omega of malls in Canada, and it feels like both a starting point and an ending place for this book. I've never lived in Edmonton, but I've spent a lot of time at West Ed – or WEM, depending on which shortened form you prefer. (I like West Ed, so please forgive me, WEMers.) I had cousins who lived around Edmonton and I had extended family in the city, and we were in Edmonton often enough that I ended up spending a fair bit of time there, right through to the present day when I first brought my own kids to see the place. West Ed is always changing. Malls, in general, are changing, as they are in the process of being displaced by online and other new forms of consumption.[1] And so even if the modernist and postmodern megamalls built in the postwar period in Canada were designed all along to make us feel nostalgic for something that we could never really put our fingers on, the narrative of shopping as a shared experience is changing.

This chapter wanders through West Edmonton Mall, interpreting it through the poetry of poet Heather Spears, in order to think about what the history of these older experiences might tell us. What is the history of malls? Where does this history point us? What is left of this history as we wend toward the future? While this book is not a historical study, but rather a cultural one first and foremost, a look back is going to help us to look at where we are and at where we might be going, whether it's a future of dead shopping malls or somewhere else entirely. One of the most interesting books on malls, *The Harvard Design School Guide to Shopping*, edited by Chuihua Judy Chung, Jeffrey Inaba, Rem Koolhaas and Sze Tsung Leong – a massive, full-colour book that focuses on the US and beyond – suggests that shopping might be the endpoint of human organization.[2] This is a world, I suppose, in which the mall takes over from the town square or the marketplace as the centre of city life, becoming the pinnacle of our social order. But if the mall as we have known it is changing or declining, then this idea might also have to change: something comes after. In this chapter, by looking at West Edmonton Mall and nodding toward where it came from, I want to suggest that we no longer have a shared or easy idea of how we shop. This change might, in its own way, lead to futures that we haven't yet imagined – maybe even better ones. The sense of nostalgia that I can't quite shake, in other words, might be a path toward the future, toward those difficult-to-find exits that many malls have hidden somewhere, just around the corner.

So then, in this chapter I present a conversation about what the forms of shopping have been like in Canada. Many people will say that the mall is essential to Canadian living – or that it is what came after the Eaton's catalogue ceased to serve its function – because the winter is really, really cold, and sometimes the summer is just too hot, and so you need somewhere indoors where you can move around. In other words, the market square moves indoors because of the shitty weather. (One time, driving near

Espanola, Ontario, I saw a billboard ad for the Espanola Mall that read, "the weather is always awesome inside!") So, to account for how malls are changing now, I read the poetry sequence "The Dolphin in the West Edmonton Mall," written by Heather Spears and published in 1988 in her book *The Word for Sand*. That book won the Governor General's Award for poetry, as well as the Pat Lowther Award. It was recently reprinted by Wolsak & Wynn, also the publisher of this book that you are holding in your hands. I first encountered these poems as an awkward and precocious undergraduate student at the University of Victoria in the late 1990s, and I always wanted to find a way to write about them because they captured, for me, something of the intangible quality of West Ed that I had experienced as a child, seeing the dolphin in its sad little tank (the sadness, of course, being my own anthropomorphization of the scene). So this chapter reads Spears' poetry alongside my own experience and a broader background, one that is about the senses of both malaise and nostalgia that exist in how, culturally, we might respond to the mall. I'd like to suggest that the mall is well aware of these feelings and seeks, in turn, to encapsulate them, to sell them back to us through the things that we might buy there.

Let's turn to "The Dolphin in the West Edmonton Mall." In the first poem in the sequence, called "Hearsay," the poet observes that the poem is something imaginary, an act of imagination. It is an imagining of the mall and, "like most imagining / it is a series of repetitives, clichés."[3] Spears' meditation on West Ed is framed within this imaginary world. It is not the "reality" of the mall in any sense, which is also necessarily true for me as I turn to write about it, to render it into words. She situates the mall within the city, which she thinks of as "flat": it is a city in which "the fields / slide fingers into the suburbs, estuaries, / the snow is melting, there's no wall / or hill between this house / and what exists out there towards the mountains." Think about the sense of direction here: instead of having humans encroach upon the open land – which is how we might usually think of it – the reverse happens. Instead, the fields "slide" back into the suburbs of the poem, and the divides between the human and the non-human are fleeting, intangible. That said, humans are portrayed as a drain on this space and the poet finds herself wondering whether the existence of the mall is somehow her "fault."

It's here that we meet the dolphin: we find it "in the centre of the West Edmonton Mall / in a small tank (I am told)." That is indeed where the dolphin – dolphins, earlier on – lived whenever I visited as a child: in one of the large corridors, in a tank, where dolphin shows would be performed at intervals throughout the day, with regular feeding times, just like at the Vancouver Aquarium except with more shopping and recirculated air. Spears, though, does not situate herself at the tank. It is only something that is reported to her, something that she is "told," reminding us that the poem is all just hearsay. That telling, that imagining, is what frames her thoughts. She turns to consider the dolphin and what the dolphin might be feeling. What, she thinks, "is so depressing / is that this brain is happy there – / ignorant of the sea." Is the dolphin happy? The poem imagines it to be. Should it be happy? No, the poem's speaker believes, the dolphin should not be happy. The situation is an outrage, a perverse misuse of intelligent animal life to entertain human animals alongside all of the other banalities that the mall has to offer us. The dolphin should be sad. But the speaker arrives at an important question: "how can I pity it / if it refuses to mourn?" she wonders. "The pleasure of the dolphin," she suggests, is disarming. It says more about her own psyche, and her expectations of misery, than anything else. Even more alarming, the happy existence that she cannot help but imagine for the dolphin in the mall is somehow redeeming of "the terrible impoverishment of the human imagination," an impoverishment that she shares, and that she locates as the first poem concludes in the mall itself, which she describes as "temporary, incarnate and forgivable." So the poem rests, in the end, upon something that we cannot decide: the mall is a terrible thing, a prison for the dolphin and for the human imagination, and yet, in its very humanity, the poet finds that she can forgive it.

—

As of this moment of writing, the biggest mall in the world is the South China Mall, opened in 2005 in Dongguan, China.[4] This huge mall is home to 7.1 million square feet of leasable shopping area (leasable square feet being one of the standard ways in which malls are measured).[5] It contains windmills, theme parks, a Venice section complete with gondolas and a replica of Paris' Arc de Triomphe. However, this mall has been radically underutilized and sat almost empty during its first decade: between 2005 and 2015 it remained for the most part mothballed, awaiting the arrival of the Chinese middle classes.[6] This mall puts me in mind of something Walter Benjamin notes of the arcades of Paris: "the arcades and *intérieurs* . . . are residues of a dream world. . . . With the destabilizing of the market economy, we begin to recognize the monuments of the bourgeoisie as ruins even before they have crumbled."[7] Benjamin's *The Arcades Project*, a massive, monumental study of Parisian architecture and culture, is another of the touchstones that anchors this book. Benjamin walks through early twentieth-century Paris and notes the arcades, built from the early mid-1800s on, architectural works that created one early form of what we might now think of as a mall. By taking what were then the new technologies of steel girders and large glassworks, and enclosing commercial streets from above so that people could stay out of the rain while shopping, developers in Paris and, soon thereafter, elsewhere hit upon a very effective way to attract people to stores. However, Benjamin notes, as developments so clearly tied to commercial activity, to a changing worldscape, the arcades are monuments to their own future ruins even as they stand. We might say exactly the same thing of a place like the South China Mall: built according to the excessive norms that are one hallmark of contemporary capitalism, it is already failing. It is a future ruin, and we can already see the process at work. We can see the processes of ruination in every mall, in fact: the crumbling concrete, the burned out lights, the dirty back corridors and the scuffed walls are all signals of what's to come. The South China Mall seems to me to be even closer to being a monument to ruin. The developers' decision to include a full-scale replica of the Arc de Triomphe connects us back to the Paris about which Benjamin writes. That monument is one that was given new prominence during the nineteenth century "Haussmannization" of Paris under Napoleon III, a process of street widening and straightening that rewrote the city and how people moved through it. These changes came, in part, as a response to the reorganization of the city through the new arcades (and also so that military forces could be swiftly moved through the city, and so that barricades wouldn't be so easy to erect by insurgent residents). So the largest mall in the world hearkens back to the arcades, to one possible beginning of the postwar malls that have popped up across North America, Asia and beyond. Its 7.1 million leasable square feet almost doubles the 3.8 million leasable square feet of West Edmonton Mall, which opened in

1981 and was, at the time, the world's largest. Notably, now eight of the ten largest malls in the world are in Asia, and four of them are in China, the country perhaps most emblematic of today's faltering turbo-capitalism.

All of these malls are very different than the nineteenth-century arcades and the Crystal Palace in London, built in 1851 – another forerunner – but they are continuous for their focus upon the experience of consumption, and the contemplation and display of goods and services. But we need to note the changes that arrived in the postwar period. The famous – or notorious – Slovenian philosopher Slavoj Žižek describes the situation as follows: "postmodern buildings tend to function as their own urban spaces (like parks inside malls, self-contained capsule worlds). . . . In this way, the public space is privatized to such an extent that it potentially suspends the very dialectical tension between private and public. A shopping mall is like a box with a world inside, separated from the outside by a plain grey wall or by dark glass panels which just reflect the outside, providing no insight or hint of what goes on within."[8] Even if this take is too simple – and is a complicated way of saying that the postmodern mall (many of those built after the 1960s, say) is a private takeover of public space – it is useful. We can think about how the suburban mall is a kind of monolith, a total space that is, maybe paradoxically, so fragmented inside that it can never be a totality. It is the sort of space in which there is no outside, an effect exacerbated by the hidden exits at West Ed. But at the same time, the inside is never a coherent space either, because it can shift so rapidly as storefronts change when leases expire and trends change.

In the second, untitled poem in Spears' sequence, the very hugeness of the mall shrinks back to the scale of the individual. The poem begins by reminding us of the dolphin: it "continues to leap" and to "disturb" the waters. It is an insistent presence in the poem. In the subsequent stanza, the individuality of the dolphin is compared to the mass of people who "watch and move away" with "curious and blank" looks on their stupefied faces. The individuality of the dolphin, in its comparison to the "blank" masses, gives us another paradox. The speaker of the poem says first that the dolphin's "despair is perfect," but then on the very next line she says, "its joy is perfect," too. It leaps in this jumbled space of consumption, a space in which everything that needs to be is "replaced" – even though, the speaker of the poem reminds us, she is not there, and all of the details are just something that an unnamed "you" has "told" to her. With this juxtaposition of individuality and the masses, and of joy and despair, both held in tension, the poem repeats the idea of the water being "disturbed" as it ends. I can't help but be struck by the word choice: when I first read that the water is disturbed, I think of a glass of water or a pool, rippling, the surface of the water lapping against an edge or shore. When the word comes back again, though, I see that there is something else going on here: the water is "disturbed" in the sense of prompting a disquiet, a sense of unease at its very existence in this space – unease that, the line suggests, is continuous, ongoing. The existence of the dolphin in the mall, in its state of both joy and despair – we cannot know which one it feels – is therefore disturbing, too. There is something more going on: the dolphin is living within the mall, within the box with a world inside of it, but it always refers us to an elsewhere. It evokes an ocean somewhere, another space, where the dolphin should be, not where the dolphin is. It is, in short, troubling.

———

In poet Lisa Robertson's essay about the thrift shop Value Village, she writes the following, somewhat elliptical statement: "We cannot fix our object. We are anxious and bored and must shop. With this scribbled grooming we thatch ourselves anew."[9] I like this sentiment; it is an unusual but insightful analysis of why we must shop. Anxiety and boredom are compelling us to repeat an action that we know won't solve our problems, but that might at least allow us to cover over our threadbare spots with new thatching. The boredom that Robertson mentions also evokes the Paris of the arcades, and especially the idea of the *flâneur* described by Benjamin – the idler who wanders the streets, taking in the city and all of the latest things. Boredom leaves us in a state of idle window-shopping (or, today, of scrolling through online shopping sites). How sedating this boredom is! How stasis-inducing are all of our anxieties that our clothes are ugly and that not enough people liked our last Facebook update or Instagram post! Quick, to the mall, for more grooming, more thatching. In the meantime, in our self-concern, the long history of exploitation – linked to if not caused by consumerism – remains something that we can neglect. Or, to put it as poet Jeff Derksen does in his poem "Compression": "I'd like to break the plate glass windows of / globalization, but I need a coffee first."[10] We are anxious to make change, but we are tired and bored – first, we must shop for a latte.

To go back to Žižek for a moment, he notes that this sort of lulling effect is right there in the architecture of the mall: "the message delivered by a building often functions as 'the return of the repressed' of the official ideology," he argues.[11] What is it that returns to us in the architecture of the mall? What is it that has been repressed? Us? Our drive to create change beyond superficial thatching? We can look at the postmodern mall, with its echoes of the arcades high up in its glassed ceilings, as a statement of the permanence of capitalism, or of its continuity. The architectural echoes want to tell us that this is a system that will last forever, and with endless growth to boot. The disappearing entrances and exits of West Edmonton Mall, however, show us something else about ideology. In this mall, either a) there is metaphorically no way out; or else b) there might be a way out, but you have to ask at the information kiosk or look at the map if you want to find out. You can't do it yourself. In the meantime, that boredom and anxiety grow, and so you have to shop. We find ourselves consuming, shopping some more because of the absence of something to do or else because we've gotten hungry. And shopping, too, keeps on shifting – those stores keep on changing – in order to keep us locked into the cycle of purchasing the very latest trends.

Heather Spears' third, again untitled, poem in her sequence on the dolphin shows us both this stasis and the ways in which a place like a mall is so easily able to contain our human actions. Here is the poem in its entirety:

And if I went down on all fours
(on my knees)
in the West Edmonton Mall
people would accept this also,
and believe that I was paid to do it
a performer
because everything is contained here
(you have told me) even obeisances,
there is even a chapel, even
a sunless beach
with nervous, fabricated tides.

The speaker's conflicted feelings – thinking back to her conflict over the dolphin, too – lead her to imagine dropping to her knees. But even such an act of despair (or reverence) is not a radical act in the mall: the mall can easily contain it; recuperate it when the bored people accept her actions, thinking that she is some sort of performer. Everything is artificial in the mall: "everything is contained here," she notes, leading us back, again, to the point that the market contains – or tries to contain – everything, making every choice a choice of shopping, of consumption. We are back to the stasis that we saw earlier: we are anxious and we are bored and so we shop. But the poem itself sticks out: it is a corrective, forcing us to think about the mall in a way that the mall itself does not invite. Spears again shows us that everything in the poem is a fabrication, something that she has made up after being "told" about the chapel in the mall and the sunless beach at the West Ed waterslides (a mall amenity which, when I was a kid, was rumoured to be infested with leeches – hurrah for urban myths). So, just maybe, the poem is an interruption, the sort of interruption that we need in order to think ourselves out of boredom and anxiety.

—

While we are probably comfortable in thinking that there is a divide between the countryside and the city, we also know – if we pause to think about it – that the divide is never so tidy. Rural spaces supply urban ones with agricultural goods, while cities contain the manufacturing, organizing and capacity that brings machinery to rural spaces, and so on. And, of course, it gets much more complicated than that: we live in a world with many different kinds of geographies, like today's export processing zones or special economic areas, areas with factories and sweatshops that lie outside of regular jurisdiction. These spaces supply hoodies and shoes for the mall, just as the giant feedlots of southern Alberta generate beef for the mall steak houses. The mall is the point where goods and services move into the hands of consumers, but these malls, too, tend to be in particular spaces: they tend to be in the suburbs. When malls were being created in their modern form, among their champions was an Austrian expatriate named Victor Gruen, mentioned earlier, who designed the first enclosed shopping mall in the United States: Southdale Center in Edina, Minnesota, opened in 1956.[12] Gruen's mall designs are positively utopic: they are supposed to be spaces for Americans to join in suburban communion. His renderings look like genuinely nice places to spend some time with other humans, and they improve upon the old department store model, which did not do a great job of serving the needs of expanded cities – organized around the automobile – after the Second World War. The reality, however, has not quite matched the possibilities that Gruen envisioned. In one of his books, he writes, "death of the city or its transfiguration – these are, in my opinion, the two alternatives before us."[13] It's not quite clear that we've arrived at one or the other, but he was very impassioned about his cause, as were others who were invested, in the postwar period, in theorizing what the mall might become.[14]

The fourth poem in Heather Spears' West Ed sequence, called "A separate place for the poor," displays the gaps and fissures between different segments of consumers. "They ought to establish / a special room for the poor / in the West Edmonton Mall," the poem begins. It would be a room "where those / who could not afford / anything / could go in order to fondle things – / furs, for example – / you said." What would this room look like? What would its effects be? Would it have the same kind of sedative role, lulling us into our compulsions to repeat, or at least mimic, the act of shopping? Would it somehow be a space that would help to create a more equal shopping centre? How would letting the poor fondle the goods help? The poem continues, clarifying that the idea comes from the "you" who speaks with the poet:

> I thought, however,
> you were going to say
> a special room for those
> who found the West Edmonton Mall
> intolerable.

The "you" notes, though, that the chapel might already serve both of these functions. But, then, this space is not quite enough either, the speaker thinks, because if you send the poor to the chapel they "would pray for money." God and manna. This poem is asking that we question the places where we consume, question who gets included and who gets left out – and how. The stories that we tell about shopping are being picked apart. Not only, of course, are some people within the population of Edmonton excluded, but so too are those in the countries that make the goods for sale. The postwar suburbs that take us to West Ed were imagined as being middle class and white, and malls like those designed by Victor Gruen were thought to be a part of those white, affluent spaces as well.[15] And so the ways that we have been taught to imagine consumption, as the poem demonstrates to us, play a role in erasing those who aren't able to join in the celebratory gestures of capitalism: if you can't afford to buy things, then you don't get to participate in this culture. Yet there is a chapel: it is a room for those who find the mall intolerable. The mall already contains its own critique, and you can buy books by Lenin without any real need to acknowledge the friction.[16] We are all, whether we are included or not, contained by the mall, contained by consumerism: even if we are excluded, the mall can sell our ideas or products. Even if we hate the mall, or are too poor to shop on credit, we can still hang out in the chapel. The mall, indeed, pushes toward being a total space in which bigger is not only better; bigger is bigger.

———

In a talk that Jeff Derksen gave in Ottawa a few years ago, he asked the following question: "would the *flâneur* move along, or would he get tasered?"[17] It's a question that has stuck with me. In that talk, Derksen was thinking about the urban spaces of contemporary Vancouver, and in particular he was thinking about how the city responded to large-scale mega-events like the 2010 Olympics. Although he was being rhetorical, events like the Olympics are ones that lead to increased "security" in the name of creating a peaceable order in a specific space for a limited amount of time (though some of those changes tend to be longer-lasting). But the question about tasering applies when we think about the mall, too. The mall is, of course, a real, material space, but it is also a space that takes us elsewhere: it is a space designed to evoke other places that consumers access when we imagine ourselves using the products that we contemplate or buy. Like how looking at a Hawaiian shirt might help us to imagine a tropical environment somewhere else, or how a dolphin might evoke an ocean. M. Jeffrey Hardwick describes a state known as the Gruen Effect, named for Victor Gruen, which is the effect of deliberately dazzling or overwhelming the senses in order to compel shoppers to keep on shopping.[18] Tasering and stunning: Is that how obedience is structured?

However, the mall does more than just stun us and transport us elsewhere, outside of our senses. The mall also, and famously, is a space that takes over the place of public spaces in postwar suburbs and in many of our cities today. Part of the imaginary nature of the mall is that it is thought of as a common space, one to which we can all go in order to enjoy the bounties of capitalism. But it is also a private space, owned and managed by companies that decide whether or not we are welcome. Behaviour that falls outside of acceptable bounds can be excluded from the mall, whether or not it is considered legal behaviour elsewhere. Sure, you could taser the Benjaminian *flâneur* while he is immersed in leisurely contemplation of the arcades-like structure of the postmodern mall, under certain circumstances. If you watch for it in the news, every now and then cases come up of people being asked to leave malls for a variety of otherwise perfectly legal actions, including breastfeeding, wearing revealing clothing, wearing politically charged or "offensive" clothing, wearing costumes (like, say, a Santa Claus outfit not sponsored by the mall) or for just walking really, really slowly. Two other malls in Edmonton, the Kingsway Mall and the City Centre Mall, have been in the news in recent years, accused of racial profiling, for asking Indigenous men to leave for no apparent reason.[19] Who controls these spaces, and what they do with that control, both emerge as important issues.

What does it mean for us socially and legally when malls come to stand in for our public spaces? There is a long historical process behind this question – one that many academics have been contemplating – about the privatization of what we once held in common. The enormous suburban malls coming to take over common, public spaces – the town square or the market-place, or even the streets running between shops, to think of a few commercial examples – is a process that we can link back to the Middle Ages in Europe. Beginning in the late Middle Ages and spanning right up until the twentieth century in England, a series of legislative measures known as the Enclosure Acts transformed lands that were previously held in the common trust into private lands, radically transforming the agricultural landscape and ushering in, among other things, the Industrial Revolution. Similar processes took place elsewhere. This legal process of taking something that was once public and rendering it private is, of course, a key challenge that environmentalists contend with today. For instance: Do we have a right to water as a common good? With many companies seeking lucrative water-sourcing contracts around the world and in Canada, this is no idle question. Similarly, we might contend that environmental measures like carbon taxes, while designed as progressive measures to halt or at least slow climate change, are also a way of privatizing the air that we breathe: Can you own polluted air? If you are responsible for the pollution, for paying for your carbon emissions, then, in a sense, you can. The mall taking over formerly public or common spaces is no simple process, in other words, and I take it quite seriously. What public, political processes can no longer happen once we meet in the mall instead of in the city square? What do we lose as political animals? (And the flip side: What, if anything, might we gain?)

The mall then is part of an ongoing process of enclosing space within the folds of the private. The arcades that so interested Walter Benjamin were first built in Paris roughly between the 1820s and the 1830s, in order to provide dry spaces for passersby. These had previously been open streets (for the most part) that were rebuilt during this time. The new technologies of iron girders and improved glassworks allowed coverings to be built overtop of the streets without sacrificing all of the light below. The stores that lined either side of the arcades benefitted from the clean and dry streets. However, arcades also quickly attracted a wide mix of behaviours that the state viewed with suspicion, like the sex work that was soon conducted in those new clean, dry places. The arcades really are fascinating; they continue to exist in places in Europe and in eastern North America and beyond.[20] As Benjamin traces the Parisian ones throughout his work, the arcades seem to be basically public spaces, but they are in the process of changing, starting with increased policing. And as shopping changes in the West over the course of the twentieth century, growing into its current forms, private property rights no longer end at the storefronts. Instead, the mall itself – with its promenades, its indoor gardens, its amusement parks, its benches, chairs and so on – starts to be built in ways that are entirely private. We enjoy these things only with the tacit permission of the owners, who often post their regulations somewhere near the mall doors. In the mall, not only is the rule of law in force, but so too is an additional set of rules, as determined by the mall's owners and managers. Think "no shirt, no shoes, no service" in the first instance, and think about the tasering of the *flâneur* in the second.

These are concerns that we can bring to Heather Spears' fifth poem in the sequence, called "The poet reconsiders visiting the West Edmonton Mall." This poem considers the mall as an enclosed space. The poem begins by noting that "half she wants to be convinced / that, in order to write about it, / she will have to see it." This possibility is one of both horror and amusement, not unlike how the poet imagines the dolphin experiencing both despair and joy. She knows that she can dislike the mall, and that she will dislike its crass consumer culture, but, nevertheless, "she is afraid / she might not dislike the West Edmonton Mall / totally and morally, as is necessary." That is to say, what if she enjoys it? Would this enjoyment signal a moral failure? Would she be corrupted by enjoying even one tiny aspect of West Ed? She goes on to compare herself to people "who dislike Child Abuse and Pornography / with such fascinated attention" – that is, to those whose dislike of disturbing parts of society signals an underlying interest in horror or in the perverse. It is an uncomfortable comparison, in that it connects shopping with child abuse and pornography. This aspect of the poem makes me, certainly, uncomfortable, but also aware of a long history of thinking about the ways in which shopping and selling goods is caught up in taboo displays, evocations of scandals and other enticements. Discomfort then is long-standing and remains.

The second stanza of Spears' poem wonders whether the main goal of West Ed is that of "seducing humanity with delight." She fears the attraction of the mall's "blazing airconditioned / skyless earthless streets" because of the questions that they raise not only about the mall, but also about herself: "What if she liked it?" she wonders. She proceeds in the following, more roundabout manner: "if she rebuked it utterly – / would she not be impoverished?" This question ends the poem. The poem turns, in my reading, on the multiple meanings of impoverishment that are possible in this moment: it is both moral and monetary, at a minimum. Rejecting the mall would mean not engaging the mall in its very materiality: it would mean rejecting her fellow humans, an act that would leave her morally impoverished. But failing to reject the mall, or even embracing it, would mean financial impoverishment – there is almost always more credit available, there is almost always more debt, and you can then buy more stuff and be parted from your hard-earned cash, both now and into the future. No matter what she does, impoverishment is a likely consequence, in other words. Neither answer – like or dislike – is satisfactory, even if it is, in the poem's terms, "necessary" that the poet dislike the mall. At this point, we are caught, both inside and outside it. The mall serves as our public space, such as it is, but it is also the subversion of that very same public space, taking it over and ruining it for us all. We find ourselves at an impasse.

—

These sorts of impasses are part of what led Jane Jacobs to hate malls. Jacobs, one of the best-known advocates for compassionate and healthy cities in the second half of the twentieth century – and especially for the Toronto in which she lived for much of her life – was no friend of the mall. In her key 1961 book, *The Death and Life of Great American Cities*, she attacks malls for, in particular, the ways in which they fragment and destroy neighbourhoods. She notes that malls can only work from an economic perspective when they hold a monopoly on the commercial spaces of North American suburbs. Malls radically affected how new suburban neighbourhoods were planned. I quite like her turns of phrase. Here is how she first puts it: "Monopolistic shopping centers and monumental cultural centers cloak, under the public relations hoohaw, the subtraction of commerce, and of culture too, from the intimate and casual life of cities."[21] That is, the way that a mall works is that it has to be the only space in a suburb at which we can shop. Streets with integrated shopping, business, cultural and residential areas tend to be few and far between in the 'burbs – suburbs have been designed in that way on purpose. Yet Jacobs notes that malls built in the postwar suburbs show us "the innate inefficiency of serving a single primary use," and suggests that malls are limited in their possibilities to the stores that have the greatest turnover.[22] Malls do not need to ensure that everything that a community needs is for sale because, instead, only the things that sell in high enough quantities are there. As a result, we end up with malls that not only take the place of common, shared public spaces but that are also defined by consumption rather than need or anything else. The results are that (sub)urban life is segmented into small pieces and that we are left with dysfunctional cities.

More recent malls, maybe in part because of this lack of diversity, have tried to incorporate more and more services and experiences. You can get married, for example, at the Mall of America. These services and other amusements have become very important to contemporary malls, all the way up to the replicas of monuments in the South China Mall. West Edmonton Mall is always changing. On West Ed's website, the "attractions" tab offers us the following: the Galaxyland amusement park, World Waterpark, Ed's Bowling, the Marine Life aquarium, the Mayfield Toyota Ice Palace (skating), Professor Wem's Adventure Golf, Dragon's Tale Blacklight Mini-Golf and a replica of Christopher Columbus' ship the *Santa Maria* (which immediately makes me think of how shopping is just one more form of colonization). These attractions are capped by the Fantasyland Hotel, a twelve-storey hotel featuring themed rooms. The possibilities are endless! (Well, they're varied, anyhow. Jacobs might note that these attractions, too, signal the death of cultural life elsewhere in the city.)

The sixth poem in Heather Spears' sequence records a trip to this smorgasbord of sensoria that never quite takes place. The poem is titled "One night they nearly went to the West Edmonton Mall."

In this poem, the pronouns shift: whereas the earlier poems used "she" throughout, now Spears shifts to "I," which invites us to identify with Spears herself on her imagined investigation of West Ed (though we shouldn't make that identification without an ongoing awareness that we're still inhabiting the world of poetry). The trip never actually takes place because, the poem begins, "it was the night the roller coaster / which is called the Mind Bender / broke like a salamander." This event, which took place on the fourteenth of June, 1986, led to the death of three roller-coaster riders. A result of faulty maintenance and construction led to the rear car of the roller coaster derailing in the middle of the second of three upside-down loops in the track. The fishtailing roller coaster failed to make it through the third loop and fell back, colliding with a concrete pillar beside the track.[23] The roller coaster, which is the largest indoor roller coaster in the world to contain three complete upside-down loops, was repaired and continues in service today. The event, however, prevents the poet from going to the mall. She states that, because of this accident, she "never saw" the dolphin and "did not kneel / in the West Edmonton Mall." But it isn't just the accident that keeps her from going. She has left the city and says that maybe she was, after all, "too angry / at the dolphin for being happy" to go. Her anger at the mall resurfaces in this poem. Her interlocutor says that "they've always called it / The Killer Mall," and she muses that she could call her suite of poems the "Killer Mall Suite" – which she does not choose to do. She may be angry, but in the end she concludes with resignation: "I do not think I would have gone," she says, had the circumstances been different. It is enough for her to know about the mall and she does not need to go there in order to understand the mix of fascination and horror that it generates in her.

The dolphin is no longer there in the tank at West Edmonton Mall. At the exhibit's peak, there were four dolphins – Howard, the last of them, died in 2005.[24] After the dolphins' deaths, sea lions were put into the tank. This process of change is, of course, not just about dolphins or sea lions, or about the things that we consume, or about fashion. It is also about how we consume things. The how is always changing. In an essay in *The Harvard Design School Guide to Shopping*, Daniel Herman makes the following prophecy: "the dead mall, already in evidence in some more prescient corners of the country" – he means the United States – "will likely be a fixture of the suburban environment in the not-too-distant future."[25] As I write, there is a Tumblr website that has gone up to document the dead Target stores of Canada.[26] The shifts and turns of consumer preference, as well as of shopping habits, is a bewilderingly difficult thing to keep up with, as Target now knows better than it did before it entered Canada. What explains these shifts? In *The Arcades Project*, Walter Benjamin ponders his own version of the question as follows: "Why does everyone share the newest thing with someone else? Presumably, in order to triumph over the dead."[27] In other words, only by having the newest thing, by being up to date, can we demonstrate that we are better, stronger than those who came before us. We need the newest thing in order to demonstrate something like progress (a term that I've long rejected), or to stand upon the shoulders of the giants who came before us, and then be able to say, "Hey! Look, my deodorant works better than yours did!" Or some such. Freud would surely be able to say something about the death drive, in analyzing why we shop and in deciphering why the ways that we shop, as well as what we shop for, are always changing. These shifting patterns signal not only the resilience of capitalism, its ability to adapt to the times, but also the possibility for capitalism itself to change, to reach its limits and to fail (which, in the scale of cosmic time, if nothing else, everything about human civilization will). At the same time, when we go to the store for the newest iPhone or any other, similar piece of semi-disposable, highly toxic junk, we also demonstrate how capital inhabits us: we are part of it at exactly that moment.

Heather Spears notes how this is a world that engulfs us in her seventh and final poem in the sequence, titled "A conceit." As in the previous poem, Spears is very ambivalent. She begins as follows:

> Here is an image:
> you are at your desk
> with your feet on your desk
> and your arms behind your head
> becoming the West Edmonton Mall.
> And you do it graciously, almost effortlessly
> your general depression
> at being human is not exclusive, you can embrace
> the worst of human failings, the most banal.

I can't quite decide if the "you" in this poem is the same as the "you" in the earlier poems in the sequence, the "you" who advises the poet and talks to her about the mall. It might be the same "you," but it also seems to expand, maybe including "us," too, as we all become the West Edmonton Mall. The poem suggests, if you will accept this expanded sense of "you," that the mall penetrates us, becomes us, or rather, that we become it. The movement is nearly effortless, as we are embedded within the culture of shopping as part of everyday life. This embedding is perhaps what allows us to "embrace / the worst of human failings." But Spears notes that this idea is entirely speculative, and she goes on:

You are also the dolphin,
incorruptible. The West Edmonton Mall
is in the distance, it never was otherwise.
You are teaching me distance, the habit of distances.

At this moment, you are, paradoxically, both the mall and the dolphin: this world embraces everything, and participation is not really a choice that we are allowed to make. The choice gets made for us, one way or another. Whether we exist inside the mall or outside of it – whether we embrace it or shun it – we nevertheless exist in some relationship to West Ed and the other malls around us, just as we exist in the nature that the speaker of Spears' poems imagines the dolphin should by rights inhabit. Spears notes that the poem is entirely a "speculation," an interesting term: it implies not only that the poem is imaginary, as before, but also that there is a possible economic sense to the life of the dolphin, too. To speculate financially is, after all, to gamble against future earnings in a world of stocks, commodity futures, derivatives and currencies, all of those zeroes and ones virtualized in the algorithms of trade today – but that nevertheless have very real, material consequences for people the world over. The mall, in this speculative mode, is both a real and an imagined space; it is, also, not reality itself. As an actual and imagined space at the same time, it highlights the dazzling variety of goods produced in today's post-Fordist economy, but it cannot contain the dolphin. The mall has a history – the arcades, the streets and the storefronts that came before, as well as, in Canada, the fur trade that led to the department stores – and it has a future. But in the present, it also has this rupture, this life in the very middle of it that signals other possibilities.

—

Not only did I visit West Edmonton Mall many times when I was young, and not only did I visit it again early on, with my kids, when I began to write this chapter, but I had another opportunity to visit as this chapter was coming to a close, when I was in Edmonton to give a talk. This trip provided me another chance to visit West Ed in an evening, and so I prevailed upon my host to take me there after giving my presentation. In particular, I wanted to check in on the section of the mall called Bourbon Street, built in the spirit of the New Orleans street of the same name. Janice Williamson wrote about this part of the mall in the early 1990s, noting that it contained some very dubious imagery of sex work, even evoking threats of sexual violence behind the false windows that decorated this strip.[28] This imagery hearkened not only to imagined fantasies of risqué life in New Orleans but also hailed back to the Parisian arcades that quickly became a hot spot for brothels and more. While Williamson noted that some of the displays had been changed after she observed and began to speak publicly about them, the overall feel of the place seemed, she felt, to be similar.

I wanted then to check out the mall once more, to take a peek at the roller coaster – which I have never been brave enough to ride, for better or worse – and to see just what was up on Bourbon Street. Edmonton's mall culture remains one of vibrant change; the zine edited by Vivek Shraya, titled *The Magnificent Malls of Edmonton*, which I mentioned at the outset of this book, had also been recently released.[29] And so: How well is the mall holding up today?

Ultimately, I couldn't tell. West Ed, I've long felt, is a mix of too many things. It is hard to decide whether it is getting more or less posh at any time. There are lots of stores there today that weren't there before – the Quebec-based chain Simons and a T & T Supermarket, for instance – and some sections of the mall have been renovated, while others look exactly the same. Bourbon Street – now shortened to BRBN Street in our post-truth, post-vowel-using era – has been given a near-total makeover. Nevertheless, in the very corner of it, close to an exit, a couple of the darkened windows that Williamson discussed do remain. My host and I sat down for a sushi dinner and discussed the mall and other malls that we've visited. We walked around afterward and she bought a book. The Galaxyland amusement park was, alas, closed by the time that we got there, so neither of us had to confront our fears of heights and roller coasters. A section of the amusement park had also just been taken apart, so we were met with a closed gate, behind which the concrete dust of whatever had been in that section of the park before still greeted us as it settled. The Mindbender roller coaster loomed large and dark in the background, its upper reaches towering up and out of sight.

And so, reasonably enough, we bowled it out. That is, we went bowling to round off the experience. While walking to the alley, I noticed that even the sea lions no longer seemed to be in the mall, or at least they weren't in the tank that night: it appeared to be completely empty. And then, walking back toward the exit, we spied the waterpark, where kayakers were using the wave pool.

There were about forty or fifty little boats taking turns riding the sunless, manufactured tides to practice the stunts that whitewater kayakers enjoy. It was, as West Edmonton Mall ever seems to be, just a little bit surreal.

Conclusion:
Retail Therapy

"Strip malls," says Madison Weiss in Todd Babiak's novel *The Garneau Block*, are "the future of world cuisine."[1] Babiak's is a rollicking novel, and it includes a number of reflections on Edmonton's suburbs and malls. What is the future of shopping? Is the future of cuisine, in fact, to be glimpsed in your local strip mall? Even though Madison Weiss is being sarcastic, some sort of truth appears to underlie this statement. I think again about Sushi Quest, our search to discover our favourite sushi restaurant in Calgary: from our quest, we seem to have learned that all of the best sushi is found in small strip mall joints – at the edges of urban spaces, where one might not expect the best food to be. So: for all of its changes, challenges and horrors, what good might the mall do? Where does it take us that we haven't been before?

Malls take us to many places, but, ultimately, I find that they often take us back home in an expanded sense of the word. When we go shopping, we can simply tell a friend that we are "going to the mall." It's an interesting phrase, "going to the mall," especially because it uses the definite article "the" instead of the indefinite article "a," which you would think would make more sense, unless we then go on to specify which mall we are talking about. But we don't need to do so: in the North American culture of the last fifty years or so, we simply say that we are going to the mall. In this context, the mall expands beyond being a specific mall: it is, instead, a sort of universal space. A universal mall, or the mall as its own universe. Our local malls, love 'em or hate 'em, connect us across time and space, because we can all go to the mall, even though we might each of us be going to different malls, different shopping spaces targeted at different demographic groups, at different socio-economic brackets, or whatever. While I don't really believe that anything is universal, there is nevertheless this universal push in our language: we all go to the mall. (Even if we don't.)

As I wend my way toward the end of this book, I find myself working my way back home, too (both literally and figuratively, as I return to my home city after time away, mostly in Montreal). The Calgary that I left when I was eighteen, and then returned to when I was thirty, no longer irks me in the way that it did when I was younger. Although my political commitments are more or less intact, I realize these days that the world is a far more complex place than I can possibly know, and I am committed, first and foremost, to developing a practice of living in as caring and kind a way as I can. When I began writing this book, I was coming out of a challenging time in my life, one full of personal and professional stresses, and I needed to make peace with myself and with my world. Writing this book has been, in its own way, a form of retail therapy – however awful that term may be – and one that has brought me back home to Alberta and to the sometimes progressive twenty-first century Calgary that I am proud to live in. This book has also brought me back to myself, in many ways. Today, Calgary is a warm place, an inviting one, with new possibilities in the air amidst serious difficulties and struggles, as we start to realize that we are going to have to do things differently in the future and, just perhaps, as we realize that we will need to work together in order to do them differently. There is a lot of anger lingering about, especially in the Trump era, but there is possibility, too. As I walk around Calgary's downtown core, I feel something different in the air, now that the city has a Muslim mayor (something that would have been just as unthinkable in my youth as a Black President of the United States – times change, thankfully), an NDP provincial government and a Trudeau back in power federally. Maybe I'm just invigorated by the political and cultural pendulum swinging back in my favour (more or less), but I can't quite feel completely gloomy about it. That is easy for me to say when I have a job, though. At a minimum, however, I don't tend to feel as angry with individuals any longer, because, increasingly, I can see that the big systems in place are made up of many flawed and beautiful individuals also trying to do their best, even though they may (and often do) fail. Somehow that eases the pressure a bit, even while it makes the world seem impossibly complex.

When I was in high school, my friends and I would often go to downtown Calgary after school. Downtown was nearby, one bus ride away, or a short C-Train ride if we chose first to walk through northwest Calgary's Kensington neighbourhood, which was formerly home to a series of used bookshops (only one of which remains today). Upon entering the city's above-ground network of buildings downtown, connected by corridors above the roads – the network known as the +15 system, or sometimes as the fifteen-plus – we would head to the food court in the buildings connected to Calgary's Eaton Centre. It was high school, and I was always hungry. Always. We would go to a local Chinese restaurant and get ginger beef, which I have been told is a Calgary specialty, within that blended Chinese-Western cuisine in which Western Canada specializes.[2] A huge serving or more of ginger beef would disappear with surprising speed down our teenaged gullets, and we would laugh and enjoy being downtown, in a space that was not quite the mall – not suburban like other malls, "suburban" already being a terrible put-down in my lexicon, well before I'd ever encountered Jane Jacobs' work – yet, at the same time, very much a space of consumption.

Thereafter, we would head next door, into the Devonian Gardens, an indoor tropical garden with tables, benches and out-of-the-way nooks designed for folks to take a break from the daily grind of office towers, during their lunch or amidst the hustle of shopping. From our hormonal, teenage point of view, Devonian Gardens was also a good place to make out, with some spectacularly secluded benches couched within the obscure corners of the foliage. As a way of ending the school day or cutting class, this practice simply could not be beat.

—

An important part of Calgary's culture, like Canada's – and not just urban Canada's, I'd like to contend, but stretching well beyond the cities in which most Canadians live – is one of shopping, of malls and of consumerism. Being able to shop and consume is one of the ways in which we mark ourselves, from the brands that we wear or boycott through to our ways of identifying our class and cultural loyalties. That's not all there is to it – far from it – but it is an important piece of a puzzle in which we are implicated, in one way or another. Take, for instance, the scene in the film *Fubar 2*, when protagonists Terry and Dean go to West

Edmonton Mall. *Fubar 2* is the sequel to the film *Fubar*, which was filmed and set largely in Calgary.[3] *Fubar* and its sequel are mockumentaries that display the lives of two "headbangers," Terry and Dean, who go about their lives in blind incomprehension, drinking, smoking and generally messing around. The first film revolves around Dean's treatment for testicular cancer, which is the source of many low-budget, ribald jokes.

In the sequel, however, Terry and Dean begin to take on more adult responsibilities. They go to work in the oil rigs of Fort McMurray, laying pipe and doing odd jobs. While there, they are exposed to the range of dodgy behaviour of which Fort Mac clichés were made before 2016's devastating fire in that community. We watch their long-time friend Tron's self-destructive, crack-fuelled death run take its course, for instance. One result of Terry and Dean's move to the oil patch is that they find themselves suddenly wealthy. They buy a big truck, get a house and more complicated love lives, and party on their time off. The pinnacle of their success is a trip that they take to West Edmonton Mall. For these relocated Calgarians, the height of arrival, the sign that they have finally made a mark, is to travel to the mall. They stay at West Ed's Fantasyland Hotel, and we see them taking in the highlights of the mall, like the waterslide park and wave pool.

For these two headbangers, the most significant cultural destination is, indeed, the mall. This moment marks the highlight of their careers in the oil patch, and we see things come apart thereafter. But the moment of pure bliss of being in the Fantasyland Hotel is complete. Terry and Dean are transfixed by the fantasies of late capitalism and, for a moment, not only do they buy into it but they also live it. It is, no matter how cynical I try to be, a pretty good moment for them. And as foolish as I may find Terry and Dean to be, the retail therapy that they seek can even work for me, some days. Let me be clear: I view shopping as basically evil, but I understand, too, how lulling it can be. My condemnation cannot be too simple or it will fail to understand the very real ways in which people like Terry or Dean interact with places like West Ed.

—

When I return to Alberta now, I am still very much aware that shopping and consumption can indeed mark class transcendence or arrival, as Terry and Dean achieve at West Ed. The spaces of shopping and consumption seem to mark their transcendence of their own old class structures every time that they are renovated, like snakes shedding their old skins. When I return to Calgary's +15 network now, some twenty years after high school, everything has changed, but everything has also stayed the same. Eaton Centre has had a complete makeover and is now linked to the TD Centre and to Holt Renfrew in a shopping centre called the Core. It is all very high end and chic. Everything is bright white inside, and the vaulted galleria above – not dissimilar to Toronto or Montreal's Eaton Centres – allows in a good quality of light, making the place welcoming enough.

Somewhat incredibly, the old Chinese food restaurant that we used to go to was still there when I first moved back to Calgary, although it is now closed. It was owned by the father of an old classmate twenty years ago, and I wondered for a while if I could track down a lost friend by asking to see the manager – but it wasn't a close friendship, and I've been learning to let such things go as time passes. The Devonian Gardens are still there too, but the plants seem sparser after the Gardens' recent renovation. There are more places to sit, more of an open-air courtyard feel to it, but far fewer places to snog. Perhaps that's on purpose. Our adolescent fumblings were, I think, very ordinary, but I imagine that many less ordinary things could have happened in those obscured corners.

I find it hard to put my finger on what it is, though, that feels different overall about the place, about the +15 network and about downtown Calgary. Of course, part of it is that I'm different now. I am older, my hair is starting to grey and I have kids of my own. But there is a different quality to this place, too. Downtown was busy then, but everything emptied out by five p.m.; now there are more people who live downtown and immediately around the city's inner core, so the hours of inhabitation shift.

One tangible difference that I can feel is that of mobile phones. I didn't have one when I was a teenager and, while some people did have them, they weren't so much the norm as they are now. This change can be meaningful in malls, which no longer tend to have clocks in them, let alone pay phones. Older malls, those from the postwar period, were often built with a central "town" square in them, which could contain clocks. Postmodern malls, on the other hand, and those that come after the postmodern, tend not only to obscure their entrances and exits, they also exist outside of time. In most malls, you will be hard-pressed to find a clock – they are now the exception rather than the rule. My experience is that clocks are disappearing from our lives – or, at least, public clocks are. I know how to check the time when I am out in the city, because I went many years without wearing a watch: billboards, parking metres and public phones are all places to look (provided that you aren't adept at reading the time based on the sun, which I am not). Schools, universities and public offices also tend to have clocks in them. I feel like there may have been one, once upon a time, in Devonian Gardens, but I'm not sure. These public timepieces are now disappearing: we are privatizing time. Everyone's mobile device comes equipped with an extremely accurate chronometer and we no longer ever need to ask anyone for the time again. As a result, we lose the ability to ask a stranger to share a valuable piece of information, but, on the other hand, mobile phones give folks a good way to avoid having undesirable exchanges in malls or on the bus.[4]

And so, without visible entrances or exits, and suspended outside of time, I walk through the labyrinth of hamster tubes that connect the shopping opportunities of downtown Calgary, bathed in the glorious prairie sunlight that streams in through the plate glass windows overhead and on all sides. While it sounds dystopic, I feel surprisingly content.

—

There is, however, still an edge of threat. One of the pieces of cultural work that got me started on this project is another film set in Calgary, *waydowntown*, released in 2000 and directed by Gary Burns.[5] It's my favourite Calgary film. It circles around the escalators and the muzak that you might hear in the elevators of downtown Calgary. Escalators always seem to me like there are puns waiting in the wings: What does it mean to escalate? Office towers not only have escalators in them – they were an important invention when they came along, in part because they allowed for three-dimensional display areas – but escalators are always connected to escalating something, too, starting with human bodies. The demand that capital always be engaged in growth – publicly traded companies have the duty of returning profits to investors, and hence constant growth is mandated – is another form of escalation. The escalation of anxiety and depression in the contemporary workplace is yet one further form of personal escalation, and the stakes always seem to be getting higher every time we go up a level.

The stakes in *waydowntown* are pretty high, too. The set-up of the film is simple enough: it stars four young twentysomething characters, Tom, Curt, Randy and Sandra, who all work together at the entertainingly named firm Mather, Mather and Mather. We never learn what the firm does, but I imagine that it's an oil patch law firm. Our four heroes occupy the bottom rungs of the corporate ladder and generally don't much care for their mind-numbing work, which seems to consist of little more than inhabiting cubicles with computers in them. Other co-workers flit through their days, including the vulnerable Vicki and the suicidal Bradley, all of who seem to be doing an absolute minimum to get by. Tom's miniature ant colony, which he keeps in his cubicle, is an obvious symbol of what these workers' lives are like. In order to cope with the tedium of their employment, as well as to demonstrate that they haven't yet succumbed to their jobs as much as the corporate shills that they see around them, the four main characters enter into a bet. The wager is a month's salary – these four young people are unattached and unburdened, it seems, by serious material concerns – and the bet is to see who can survive indoors for the longest. It is possible for them to live indoors, the film explains, because they live in a city in which the condominium towers are connected to the office towers, which are in turn connected to the shopping centres, restaurants and entertainment complexes. The film never explicitly names it, but the city is very obviously Calgary, from the radio station heard playing during the film's opening credits – Calgary's CJAY92 – to the Calgary Tower, visible in several shots, and to the recognizable map of the downtown core.

When we join our characters, they have already been following their wager for some time: it is day twenty-four of their indoor confinement. The action takes place, for the most part, over a single lunch hour. It is the day on which company founder Mr. Mather will be retiring, and there is a party in his honour scheduled for the afternoon. Each of the film's main characters is suffering different stresses as a result of her or his self-imposed incarceration inside the mall/office/home complex of downtown Calgary. Tom is increasingly worried that he has become a shallow, callous person who is inured to the suffering of others. He is the film's protagonist, as he provides the voice-over narration and we follow him most closely. He notes, for instance, that he no longer even breaks stride when people collide while looking at their phones or papers. He is sarcastic and rude to others, and, at least at first, feels little apparent guilt when he picks up a woman who works in a downtown shop and, as a result, upsets the woman's existing boyfriend. He is also unable to feel sympathy for "sadly I'm Bradley," his suicidal cubicle neighbour. Bradley shows us one likely future for Tom himself, although Tom does not recognize it. At about the midpoint of his seemingly meaningless career – Tom says to him that he's "halfway home" – Bradley appears to have achieved nothing thus far, and he brings a two-litre plastic pop bottle filled with marbles into the office, a bottle that should be weighty enough to break the shatterproof glass of the office and allow him to jump to his death. Marble-filled bottles provide a clue to the name of the film itself: the worker who serves Tom his morning coffee asks him, "What's the difference between the 15-plus and a bottle of marbles?" Tom, who doesn't seem to care, doesn't answer. The server eventually replies that the +15 takes you downtown, but that the bottle of marbles takes you "waydowntown," which is a way for him to refer to the suicide of depressed office workers who have been using the marble-filled bottle trick for some time. Tom, who is becoming worried about his own failings, realizes through the telling of this "joke" that Bradley's bottle of marbles is a sign (one among many) that he is about to attempt suicide, and he rushes off to intervene. But Tom's dawning self-awareness does not end there: he is also concerned about how he has been living in a weed-induced, mildly stoned state in which he has begun to have delusions – he imagines in one scene, for instance, a giant fish devouring his leg. The film is shot with yellow and orange tones, highlighting the artificiality of the indoors and making Tom, like most of the characters, appear distinctly sallow.

Curt's sufferings are sexual. It turns out that he has previously won a similar competition while a student at Ottawa's Carleton University. His challenge is what to do with his libido. He reveals to Tom that although he is engaged, his fiancée will not have sex with him until they are married. Their relationship, Curt shares, is an open one, allowing him to have casual sex with others. He has not, however, been "getting any," as he puts it. His reputation for being smarmy seems well deserved and his relationship, as he depicts it, is not a terribly happy one. He embarks upon a lunch-hour tryst with co-worker Vicki, whose own engagement has been dragging on unhappily for about the same length of time as Curt's. They go to the office women's bathroom in order to have sex, only to be discovered by their other co-workers. Curt is unpleasant, perhaps superficially attractive, constantly chews gum and, throughout the film, appears to be smug and knowing.

Randy, conversely, seems to have his confidence shattered by the experience of being confined to the indoors. He spends his lunch hour hanging out with his friend Phil, a security guard. Randy wonders aloud to Phil whether he is becoming a bad person. When Sandra presents him with a request from the company to go and pick up a plaque to give to Mr. Mather for his retirement, he complains that the location of the plaque store requires that he go outdoors. He then convinces Phil to take him there inside a wheeled garbage can so that he does not, technically, go outside and hence lose the bet.

Sandra, finally, is totally losing it after all of the time confined to the indoors. Assigned to follow company founder Mr. Mather during the lunch hour – he is an elderly kleptomaniac who wanders the stores of downtown, lifting whatever suits his fancy – she appears to suffer the most from the environmental conditions of the mall. Early in the film, Tom observes to her that the air in downtown Calgary is all recycled, and she begins to show signs of asphyxiating from the air conditioning. As the camera follows Sandra, individual shots zoom in on air vents, some of them dubbed over with the sounds of muffled screams. In a suppressed panic, Sandra becomes more and more distraught, at one point walking into a magazine store and stealing a perfume sample page so that she can smell something more pleasant. Later, as she tracks Mr. Mather, she finds herself at one point twirling a revolving door to the outside so that she can catch brief gasps of outdoor air.

The wager is taking its psychological toll; everyone, in short, is falling apart. The film turns increasingly surreal as Tom begins to float along the mall corridors. His clothes change inexplicably from one shot to the next, as do Sandra's, suggesting that this single lunch hour is representative of every lunch hour, every single day in the office the same as every other. This bizarre lunch hour in the mall connected to their shared office tower seems to separate these characters evermore from reality. At one point, Tom follows Kathy, the woman he has just picked up and who works in the mall, as she runs in distress after her boyfriend, Paul. Paul is on the ground, and the film sets us up to wonder if he has jumped to his death. Tom stops himself at the door to the mall, just before going outside, where Paul lies on the ground, immobile. Although it turns out to be a case of simple malaise – Paul is lying on the ground in his sorrows because of his girlfriend's wandering affections – Tom wonders if he is losing it in his failure to go outside and help a fellow human being. Indeed, we can see in this moment that his confinement within the mall and downtown seems to be separating him and his peers from reality.

—

Does the experience of being in the mall, or the experience of malling, of getting malled, remove us from reality or connect us to the bizarre dimensions of super-reality that we inhabit in our posthuman moment today? Walking around downtown Calgary seems to confirm that the world is a strange one: the plants grow indoors, even up the walls – as opposed to in the largely concrete world outside – the time is always the perpetual present and you have to go downstairs, into the subconscious levels of the mall's strata, in order to find an exit.

I depart from the most obvious parts of the +15 system in my meandering. In the corners of the network, you will find homeless people walking, staying indoors and away from the heat or the cold, depending on the season. The Arts Commons connects to the Convention Centre and to the Glenbow Museum, where the corridors exist in a state of perpetual dim light. While Calgary starts to show early signs of recovering – or at least stabilizing – from a full-blown recession connected to the collapse of oil prices, shops are still going out of business, and closed storefronts are more and more common. For the past while, it has seemed that, no matter what the government, banks and businesses try, the economy will have no simple fix. "Consumer confidence," as they call it, is low, and more people are in vulnerable states than at any other time in living memory. The suicide rate in Alberta jumped by thirty per cent in 2015.[6] I have friends who are out of work, looking to find their next opportunity – and some not actually bothering, saying that there's no point. Some of these folks are finding new ways to contribute to their communities outside of formal employment. In the meantime, the government is touting a version of a Keynesian model for fixing the issue through infrastructure works. In the medium term, there is confidence that the price of oil will go back up – it has started, perhaps, to turn the corner, or at least to hit bottom. In the longer term, however, it seems to me that we are all, at some level, aware of the validity of the *Adbusters*-esque critique that the economy is based upon unsustainable models of growth and will need to change at a fundamental level. Whether people are walking around in a stupor of unemployment or in the daze of the hyper-consumptive zombie, things are not quite right and, either way, you can see it on display in the mall.

—

The lunch hour of the four main characters of *waydowntown* feels evermore out of control and veers toward the point of collapse. As the film becomes yet more surreal, Tom imagines that downtown Calgary has been picked up by an evil comic book–style supervillain and taken into space. A recurrent, non-speaking figure, a superhero in spandex and a cape with a pink triangle on his chest, runs through downtown Calgary, and things return to

Earth – back to normal – once again. Piece by piece, however, a new order emerges: our four main characters have cracked and are making changes. Curt phones his fiancée to suggest to her that maybe it's time to finally go ahead and get married; he is, at least on the surface of things, symbolically ready to grow up in spite of his faults. Tom finds Bradley in time to witness the failure of his suicide attempt; the bottle of marbles fails to break the plate glass of the office tower window, bouncing back and hitting Bradley in the head. Tom consoles him, taking responsibility for his own lack of concern for his co-worker's well-being. Tom then takes the bottle of marbles and places it in the box that was supposed to contain a valuable vase to be given to Mr. Mather at the retirement party. He gives the flowers that were also supposed to be for his boss to the still-distraught Vicki and walks away from the office, to the outdoors, never to return.

Sandra, in turn, decides to say a symbolic "fuck it" to the contest (she literally says it, too) and opts to go outside. Once she's there, she spots Phil wheeling Randy, inside his garbage can, over to the plaque and trophy store. She takes the garbage can from Phil and wheels Randy over to a dumpster, where she leaves him. They are both, as a result, out of the contest. It is, if anyone is still keeping track, the smarmy Curt who wins, but the cost is the loss of everyone's respect and friendship.

As the film moves toward its conclusion, a very interesting technical shift tells us as much about the world of *waydowntown* as any of its characters' actions. Sandra is the first whom we see going outside. The horrid indoor air has gotten the best of her and she steps out through a set of doors (ones that look to me like those in front of the old cosmetics counter at the Bay's downtown store) and onto the street. As she does so, filmmaker Gary Burns appears to make a very conscious choice to alter the appearance of the film (which is shot on video⁷). Whereas the film has had a distinctly orange hue up to this point, with the characters looking very unwell indoors, the look of the film is distinctly different outdoors. All of a sudden, the colours of the film jump out and we see what looks, at first, to be a much more vivid appearance of the human form on screen. This seeming relief, however, is short-lived: after a few seconds outside, Sandra looks around and sees cars and buses driving on the downtown streets. The film's appearance changes again to the sort of grainy, blue-and-grey-toned look that characterizes filmic realism as she realizes that the exhaust spewing from the vehicles and buildings is rendering the air just as sickly as the indoor environment. Sandra returns to the office (and back to the orange tones) and declares to Tom that both she and Randy are out of the contest. Tom, too, is subject to the same initial change in the film's appearance when he leaves the office and then walks outside at the very end, though shots of him do not progress to the grainy blue-grey: they continue to invoke a richer-hued, more healthful image. He steps into the air and takes a breath. Then, suddenly, a bottle of marbles explodes on the ground next to him. He looks up and the film freezes in its final shot. While frozen, the shot progressively zooms in toward Tom's face and, finally, reflected in his eye, we see a body falling. Some critics have seen the falling body as being that of Mr. Mather, who has just been given the bottle by Tom in lieu of his expected retirement gift: Mr. Mather has, after many years, finally made a macabre escape.⁸ Before he can fall, though, and while he is still reflected in Tom's eye, we see the silhouetted figure of the superhero return to catch the body and zoom off to safety. At this moment, the film ends.

In the final analysis, it is difficult to decide: Does Tom return to reality, to reason and balance, when he leaves his sickening office job and the interminable mall? His voice-over narration suggests that may be the case. Or do we all live within a surreal or super-real world in which malls and office towers are only one escalating part? Although Tom is now outside, the super-hero figure has not disappeared; in fact, he is more important than ever. The air outside, as we have learned, is hardly better than the air indoors. And even though the appearance of the film has changed for the outdoor shots, it's not as though the shots are, in themselves, any more "real" than those that came before: we're still in the world of the film, not in the world itself. So even though Tom, Sandra and Randy have all stepped back into the outdoors and left the mall, and even though Curt is making sym-bolic plans to get on with his life, they are still confined within the frame of the film itself – and in turn by the various shapes and strictures of the market practices surrounding the cinema (grants, production, distribution and so on), all of which ensure that while the system that we inhabit may not be a total one, it certainly is a totalizing one that contains us so very well in most of our day-to-day actions.

———

This book ends some two years before it begins, on December 26th, 2012. Boxing Day again, but a different year. I moved back to Calgary in 2009 (with my year in Montreal an out-and-back journey). It's taken me more than a few years to recalibrate myself to being home, but I think that I'm much closer now than I was when this project started. On Boxing Day 2012, I went not to Chi-nook Centre, where I started this book with my notebook and pen, but rather to Marlborough Mall, an unassuming mall in the northeast of Calgary. Marlborough Mall is notable mostly for its

Walmart and its dollar stores: it is a low-cost, working-class mall close to where my partner's mother lives.

We were there for an Idle No More rally, for one of the flash mobs held in malls across Canada and the US in 2012 and into 2013 and beyond.[9] Late in his book *The Reason You Walk*, Anishinaabe musician, journalist, writer and NDP provincial politician Wab Kinew describes going to a parallel event on the same day in Winnipeg:

> On Boxing Day, Lisa [his partner] and I went to the mall. Idle No More Winnipeg had called for a flash mob round dance, an urban take on the traditional friendship dance of the Plains.
>
> The mall was crowded enough, but the halls were impassable as we approached the main square. Pushing through the wall of people, I saw familiar faces smiling and mouthing hellos. Christmas greetings were exchanged....
>
> When the time came, I found my way to a group of singers I had travelled with on the powwow trail in my late teens and early twenties. The drums kicked in one after another, falling into the *boom-chicka-boom* rhythm of the round dance.
>
> One singer kicked out a lead, and all of the other singers grabbed it, following the melody he had set, with an explosion of sound. Chills went up my spine. As I sang, I looked around at hundreds of people joining hands and sidestepping to their left in time with the beat.
>
> I felt the power around me. The power of the drums. The power of the voices. The power of community....
>
> This, to me, is the key achievement of Idle No More – the flash mob round dance. Our cultures were marching

back into the public spaces and the national collective conscience. We are still here. We are still strong. We are never going away. Don't call it a comeback – we've been here for years.[10]

Our Boxing Day experience was similar, though different in important ways. The event in Calgary's northeast was loud, rowdy and celebratory. Held immediately next to the mall's food court, a few hundred people flocked together with seeming spontaneity, prompting the security guards to throw up their hands and just go with it. Drummers began a beat and singers followed suit. There was a round dance, but, because of both the set up of the mall and the sheer number of people pressed into a small space, it was difficult to keep moving. Many simply clustered around the core circle of dancers, cheering along. The event wasn't without its tensions: a man in a wheelchair, for instance, tried to get through the crowd, frustrated by the obstruction of the ramp that he needed to access in order to proceed. But on the whole it was a celebratory and defiant atmosphere, and my daughters, taking turns up on my shoulders, took it all in. Everyone whooped and hollered and drummed and then, just as quickly, dispersed. A few weeks later, I participated in another round dance in front of Calgary's City Hall; later in the winter, I joined an Idle No More rally in Edmonton, at the Provincial Legislature. I followed along and supported while I could, but the event in the mall on Boxing Day is the one that has stuck with me.

Kinew, in his description, is part of the community, part of the crowd: he is among friends and depicts himself as being greeted by others as such. I did not share such an easy communion with folks on that day, though it was an important step. Although my partner is a member of the Métis Nation of Alberta, I am not of

Indigenous heritage, and so I want to be respectful in how I strive to be an ally to Indigenous struggles – these struggles are important ones to me because I have many Métis relations. The challenge remains as to how best to participate in and be part of community in late capitalist culture – and particularly while spending time in the mall. The day was, in my view, part of choosing to reconnect with Calgary in very specific ways.

Idle No More situated a huge part of its work specifically in malls. It was and is a large-scale pan-Indigenous mobilization that has focused on the ways in which Indigenous peoples and allies forge communities and political movements in the here and now. The here and now was, I think, well served by being addressed in malls across North America. There were tensions, with reports that some malls did not wish to have Indigenous protests hosted there – not dissimilarly to how the Mall of America was recently criticized for banning a Black Lives Matter rally (the mall owners observed, as per the long history of Enclosure, that because it is private property they have the right to dictate how the space is used).[11] But the Idle No More round dances took place, and community was generated through the connections made and affirmed in malls.

Can we come to the mall and find community today? Bizarrely, and against the expectations with which I began this book, it seems to me that, in limited ways, we can. The nightmare scenario of *waydowntown* exists in contrast to the Idle No More flash mob. While the owners have the "right" to dictate how we exist in those spaces that does not mean that we have to obey those dictates. I hope that we do obey some of the rules: when I visited the Mall of America, for instance, I approved of the signs banning guns in the mall. But we might take a page from the French thinker Michel de Certeau, who argues in *The Practice of Everyday Life* that, rather than seeing capitalist society just as a carceral world of regulations and social norms that are enforced both violently and more subtly, we can also see it as a world of transgression, one in which we make use of spaces in ways that were never anticipated. De Certeau is keen on finding small acts of sabotage in the daily operations of workers, in discovering how people deploy strategies and tactics that lead to change, in finding the cracks in the system that still allow for creativity to flow.[12] The public squares of earlier cities were not exactly spaces of freedom either: many gatherings and protests in public spaces have ended with police crackdowns. But when an Idle No More flash mob suddenly shows up at the mall? It may be a violation of mall policy – perhaps. The round dance has already started, though, and it's too late to stop it now. Although we seem to be consuming our planet to its grave, community is forming in the mall, and the mall is and will remain a site of complex contestation. For all of the control of contemporary capitalist and consumerist culture, humans are too wonderful, too divergent, too beautiful for us to be able to predict everything perfectly in advance. And it's a good thing, too. Among the many reasons that this is so, it means that, when I have the choice between a blue tie or a red tie, as Tom gets to choose in his corporate job in *waydowntown*, I can choose neither, find the exit, and walk out and into the sun.

In the End:
The Future

It is, of course, impossible to predict what the futures of shopping, consumption and consumerism are going to look like. In the United States, malls seem to be dying. In Canada that seems to be a bit less true, but at the same time, erstwhile major stores do periodically go under (think Eaton's, Target and, in the news right now, the struggles of Sears). Perhaps it will be a future of drones humming through the air, quietly dropping our online orders off at our doorsteps, or a future of online everything, or a future of bland, faceless outlet stores.

The future as predicted by Margaret Atwood, for instance, is a bleak one. In her dystopic MaddAddam trilogy, one of the most important things to destroy human society is consumerism. In particular, people's ever-growing drive toward longer, more superficially beautiful lives takes a tremendous toll on society. Endless corporations devoted to quack beauty cares and the quest for immortality decimate environments, landscapes, the social order and, ultimately, the world as we have known it. The segregation between the "haves," in their corporate compounds, and the "have-nots," in what Atwood terms the "pleeblands," is an extrapolation from life today that demonstrates the extent to which our habits of consumption stratify, divide and kill us.

My own fears are, more specifically, that environmental destruction wrought by our consumptive practices may be our undoing. Various statistics suggest that we would need multiple Earths to sustain us if everyone consumed like a North American, a Canadian or an Albertan. What do we do, however, with this knowledge? While recognizing the sometimes awful, yet sometimes also beautiful practices that come from consuming and shopping in Canada, it is abundantly clear to me, after doing this work, that our habits will need to change, and change quite radically, too. There needs to be a future between Kraft Dinner and Walmart for the many, and charcuterie boards and designer shoes for the few. What this change will look like, however, is up to us.

Acknowledgements

Many thanks are due to the people who have supported me during the time of this project. None of them, however, should be held liable: the shortcomings of this work are entirely my own. At Wolsak and Wynn, I would like to thank Noelle Allen for her acumen, support and fine guiding hand. Andrew Wilmot performed magic in editing the manuscript. The initial essay that led to this book, an academic essay on West Edmonton Mall, appeared in the book *Literature and the Glocal City: Reshaping the English Canadian Imaginary* (Routledge, 2014). Thanks to Heather Spears for encouraging my analysis of her poetry, which enabled me to write that chapter. Thank you to Ana María Fraile-Marcos for her astute editorial work on that project. An earlier version of the chapter on Whitehorse appeared in the magazine *Eighteen Bridges* (spring/summer 2017), and I would like to thank Curtis Gillespie for his support there. Talks in preparation for this book were given in Edmonton, Fredericton, Montreal and Waterloo, as well as Salamanca and Vigo, Spain. Thank you to Imre Szeman, Sheena Wilson, Marie Carrière, David Leahy, Will Straw, Belén Martin-Lucas and Pilar Cuder-Dominguez for their work in organizing and hosting those events, as well as to audiences who generously shared their thoughts and ideas. Thank you to

Mount Royal University and to the McGill Institute for the Study of Canada's Eakin Visiting Fellowship in Canadian Studies. Sarah D'Onofrio's work as my Research Assistant was invaluable. Thank you also to my students in Canadian Studies 405 at McGill and English 4472 at Mount Royal University for their very thoughtful engagement.

For ongoing conversations, support, mentorship and kindness, thank you to everyone in my academic communities. I profoundly respect the quiet everyday work that you do, as well as the generosity of spirit that you maintain in spite of sometimes long odds. I have nothing but gratitude for you every day. Many specific conversations helped this project along, and I'm happy to acknowledge that ones that I had with Paul Barrett, derek beaulieu, Christian Bök, Andrew Burke, Daniel Coleman, Lisa Cooke, Jane Drover, Nicolas Field, Shoshannah Ganz, Avi Grenadier, Helen Hajnoczky, Richard Harrison, David and Gail Jardine, Hannah MacGregor, Heather Milne and Naava Smolash directly helped my thinking. Thank you, folks.

I couldn't imagine having completed this work without all of my friends and family. Gratitude is due to you all. Thank you, Patti and Bruce, for valiantly offering to be my Virgilian guides to the underworld of the mall – and for all else, every day. Thank you to my parents, Keith and Debbie, for taking me to the mall when I was a child and then when I was a surly teenager. It must have taken a lot of patience. Thanks to Beth and Simon for laughter, pie, beers and cheers. To Alexandra and Clementine, I would like to share my gratitude for helping me to see the world from a new perspective. Aubrey Jean Hanson is an amazing human being who helps me to become a better one in turn.

Endnotes

PREFACE

1   Jackie Wattles, "Stores are closing at an epic pace," *CNN Money*, 22 April 2017, http://money.cnn.com/2017/04/22/news/credit-suisse-retail/index.html.

2   "Calgary downtown vacancy rate moving toward 25%," *CBC News*, 1 June 2016, http://www.cbc.ca/news/canada/calgary/office-space-vacancy-rising-1.3611785.

3   Vivek Shraya, "If These Malls Could Talk," *vivekshraya.com*, 15 May 2015, https://vivekshraya.com/essays/if-these-malls-could-talk/.

INTRODUCTION: CHINOOK CENTRE

1   Kayla Butler, "A crowd larger than Red Deer hits up Calgary's Chinook mall for Boxing Day," *660 News*, 27 December 2014.

2   At present, Calgary's footprint is 848 square kilometres and the population is a little bit over 1.2 million residents (a bit more than 1,415 people per square kilometre). New York City, in turn, occupies 790 square kilometres and has a population of a bit over 8.5 million (10,759 people per square kilometre). These statistics are widely available online.

3   I will come back to this point later, but shopping malls surface a few times in Jane Jacobs' monumental book, *The Death and Life of Great American Cities* (New York: Vintage, 1961).

4   I also like to take cues from Halberstam, whose *The Queer Art of Failure* (Durham, NC: Duke University Press 2011) is a romp through films like *Dude, Where's My Car?* and TV series like *Spongebob Squrepants*. Halberstam celebrates the joy to be found in failing to live up to one's roles because of the non-normative possibilities that result, and I think that, albeit in limited ways, I might do so too at times.

5   See the April 2016 issue of *Alberta Views* on this subject.

6   *Mallrats*, prod. Caldecot Chubb, dir. Kevin Smith, 94 minutes, View Askew, 1995, DVD. As I write, a sequel TV series, *Mallbrats*, is apparently in production.

7   For instance, see David Uberti, "The death of the American mall," *Guardian*, 19 June 2014, https://www.theguardian.com/cities/2014/jun/19/-sp-death -of-the-american-shopping-mall; Jonathan Glancey, "The death of the US shopping mall," *BBC Culture*, 21 October 2014, http://www.bbc.com/culture /story/20140411-is-the-shopping-mall-dead; Nelson D. Schwartz, "The Economics (and Nostalgia) of Dead Malls," *New York Times*, 3 January 2015, https://www.nytimes.com/2015/01/04/business/the-economics-and-nostalgia-of-dead-malls.html; Hayley Peterson, "America's Shopping Malls are Dying a Slow, Ugly Death," *Business Insider*, 31 January 2014, http://www .businessinsider.com/shopping-malls-are-going-extinct-2014-1; and so on. There are also academic studies of the phenomenon, from the disciplines of business and marketing through to sociology and cultural studies.

8   Donica Belisle, *Retail Nation: Department Stores and the Making of Modern Canada* (Vancouver: UBC Press, 2011).

9   The concept of false consciousness is a generally derided element of the Marxist lexicon, sometimes falsely attributed to Marx himself. Effectively, denouncing someone for inhabiting false consciousness is a way of saying that someone is unable to understand the real relations that they inhabit because ideology is blinding them. One could go to, for instance, Terry Eagleton's book *Ideology: An Introduction* (London: Verso, 1991) or Slavoj Žižek's *Mapping Ideology* (London: Verso, 1995) in order to get into the debates behind this point.

10 Douglas Rushkoff, *Coercion: Why We Listen to What "They" Say* (New York: Riverhead, 1999), 75–76.

11 My thanks to Christian Bök for making this observation in conversation.

THE MALL VS. THE OUTDOORS: CROSSIRON MILLS

1   Weyman Chan, *Chinese Blue* (Vancouver: Talonbooks, 2012), 60.

2   At this time, the employee shuttle remains, and there is, as of September 2015, transit available from the Airdrie public transit service.

3   The information about the mall is taken directly from their website: crossironmills.com.

4   Aritha van Herk, *Mavericks: An Incorrigible History of Alberta* (Toronto: Penguin, 2001), 2.

5   Ibid., 5.

6   Ibid., 316.

7   Sinclair Ross, *As For Me and My House* (1941; Toronto: McClelland & Stewart, 2008), 3.

8   Ibid., 97.

9   Ibid., 10.

10 Ibid., 20.

11 Ibid., 90.

12 Ibid., 231.

13 David Schindler, "Foreword," *Eau Canada: The Future of Canada's Water*, ed. Karen Bakker (Vancouver: UBC Press, 2007), xiii; John Sprague, "Great Wet North? Canada's Myth of Water Abundance," *Eau Canada*, 24; 29–30.

14 See Theodore Horbulyk, "Liquid Gold? Water Markets in Canada," *Eau Canada*, 205–18.

15 See "Alberta Water Policy Data," *The Living Water Project*, waterpolicy.ca, 2012, http://www.waterpolicy.ca/alberta-water-policy.

16 See "Canada's Rivers at Risk: Environmental Flows and Canada's Freshwater Future," *World Wildlife Fund*, 15 October 2009, http://www.wwf.ca/?4820.

17 This sequence of events is discussed in Renata D'Aliesio, "Tapped Out: The Clash Over Alberta's Water Series: Part One of Three," *Calgary Herald*, 1 December 2007, A19–20.

18 I'll limit myself to recommending one article: Cheryl Lousley, "'Hosanna Da, Our Home on Natives' Land': Environmental Justice and Democracy in Thomas King's *Green Grass, Running Water*," *Essays on Canadian Writing* 81 (2004), 17–44.

19 Robert Kroetsch, *Alberta*, 2nd ed. (Edmonton: NeWest Press, 1993), 12.

20 Thomas King, *Green Grass, Running Water* (Toronto: HarperCollins, 1993), 111.

21 Ibid., 208, 267, 271.

22 Ibid., 376.

23 Ibid., 118.

24 Ibid., 352.

25 Naomi Klein, *This Changes Everything: Capitalism vs. the Climate* (Toronto: Knopf, 2014).

26 Allan Stoekl, *Bataille's Peak: Energy, Religion, Postsustainability* (Minneapolis: University of Minnesota Press, 2007), xvii, 33.

27 Ibid., 123.

28 Zygmunt Bauman, *Consuming Life* (Cambridge: Polity Press, 2007), 38.

29 Linda Hutcheon, *Splitting Images: Contemporary Canadian Ironies* (Toronto: Oxford University Press, 1991), vii.

NO WAY OUT: EATON CENTRE VS. HONEST ED'S

1 Émile Zola, *The Ladies' Paradise*, trans. Brian Nelson (1883; Oxford: Oxford University Press, 1995), 18, 76.

2 Godfrey M. Lebhar, *The Chain Store – Boon or Bane?* (New York: Harper & Brothers, 1932), 4, 201.

3 The classic and indispensable study is Harold Innis, *The Fur Trade in Canada* (1930; Toronto: University of Toronto Press, 1977). Innis informs much of early Canadian economic theory, especially the staples thesis as developed in

Mel H. Watkins, "A Staple Theory of Economic Growth," *Staples and Beyond: Selected Writings of Mel Watkins*, eds. Hugh Grant and David A. Wolfe (1963; Montreal and Kingston: McGill-Queen's University Press, 2006), 5–29. From a similar era, see also W.T. Easterbrook and Hugh G.J. Aitken, *Canadian Economic History* (Toronto: Macmillan, 1956).

4   Since I wrote this chapter, the store's current location has closed. They exist online at the moment and anticipate finding a new storefront soon.

5   Donica Belisle, *Retail Nation: Department Stores and the Making of Modern Canada* (Vancouver: UBC Press, 2011), 39.

6   See for instance (and to focus on one of the more recent publications) Bruce Allen Kopytek, *Eaton's: The Trans-Canada Store* (Charleston: History Press, 2014). There is a large literature around Eaton's, and every history of department stores or of retail in Canada necessarily addresses the store's rise and fall in some depth.

7   See the description by Richard Rhodes in "Michael Snow: The Public Commissions," *The Michael Snow Project: Visual Art, 1951–1993*, ed. Dennis Reid (Toronto: Art Gallery of Ontario / Knopf, 1994), 490.

8   That case was decided in the Ontario Court of High Justice, citation 70 CPR (2d) 105, [1982] OJ No 3645.

9   Fredric Jameson, *Postmodernism: Or, The Cultural Logic of Late Capitalism* (Durham, NC: Duke University Press, 1991), 20, 40.

10 See M. Jeffrey Hardwick, *Mall Maker: Victor Gruen, Architect of an American Dream* (Philadelphia: University of Pennsylvania Press, 2003), 162 and following.

11 Throughout this book, I have by and large tried to avoid making too-easy comparisons between churches and malls – often called today's new places of worship or whatever – but here and there the comparisons do seem apt. The age-old practice of comparing the two is I think usefully discussed in John Fiske's old but still readable 1989 essay "Shopping for Pleasure: Malls, Power, and Resistance," *The Consumer Society Reader*, eds. Juliet B. Schor and Douglas B. Holt (New York: New Press, 2000), 306–28, an essay that seems to divide readers with regard to whether shopping can ever be seen as an empowering gendered practice.

12 See Jack Batten, *Honest Ed's Story: The Crazy Rags to Riches Story of Ed Mirvish* (Toronto: Doubleday Canada, 1972).

13 Pico Iyer, *The Global Soul: Jet Lag, Shopping Malls, and the Search for Home* (London: Bloomsbury, 2000), 141.

14 Bryan Lee O'Malley, *Scott Pilgrim & The Infinite Sadness* (Portland: Oni Press, 2006).

15 Colin Perkel, "Man admits shooting up Eaton Centre food court, says it wasn't planned," *Globe and Mail*, 10 October 2014, https://www.theglobeandmail .com/news/toronto/man-admits-shooting-up-eaton-centre-mall-food-court -but-says-it-wasnt-planned/article21063246/.

16   "Life sentence for Jane Creba murder," *CBC News*, 22 December 2009, http://
www.cbc.ca/news/canada/toronto/life-sentence-for-jane-creba-murder
-1.845433.

17   Bryan Lee O'Malley, *Scott Pilgrim Gets It Together* (Portland: Oni Press, 2007).

18   Even Justin Bieber took part in this celebration of Santa. See CBC News' slow-
news-day coverage: "Justin Bieber takes selfie with Fashion Santa at Yorkdale,"
CBC News, 19 December 2015, http://www.cbc.ca/news/canada/toronto
/bieber-selfie-fashion-selfie-1.3373624.

19   David Hall, "A True Urban Centre: Collaborative Community Problem-Solving
and the Dufferin Mall," *Community Stories* (Toronto: Caledon Institute for Social
Policy, 1997), 6.

BUYING MEMORIES: THE MAIN, THE MONTREAL FORUM AND THE UNDERGROUND CITY

1   For the interested: the piece is "La grande allée à Giverny," painted in 1900.

2   Roch Carrier, *The Hockey Sweater*, trans. Sheila Fischman (Toronto: Tundra
Books, 1979); *The Sweater*, dir. Sheldon Cohen, 10 minutes, National Film
Board, 1980.

3   Jean-Claude Germain, "Incomparable Panache," *Geist* 99 (2015), 34. From his
book *Of Jesuits and Bohemians*, trans. Donald Winkler (Montreal: Véhicule, 2014).

4   Mordecai Richler, *The Street* (1969; Toronto: Penguin, 1985), 65–66. Richler
describes the area similarly in *Son of a Smaller Hero* (1955; Toronto: McClelland
& Stewart, 2002), 3–4.

5   M. G. Vassanji, *Mordecai Richler* (Toronto: Penguin, 2009), 19.

6   Heather O'Neill, "Putting Together a Robot Without an Instruction Manual,"
Lullabies for Little Criminals (New York: Harper Perennial, 2006), 9.

7   Jason Freure, "A 19-Year-Old's Referendum: An Interview with Heather
O'Neill," supplement, *Puritan* (Summer 2015), http://puritan-magazine.com
/a-19-year-olds-referendum-an-interview-with-heather-oneill/.

8   Heather O'Neill, *Lullabies for Little Criminals* (New York: Harper Perennial,
2006), 5–6.

9   Ibid., 7.

10   Ibid., 322.

11   O'Neill, *The Girl Who Was Saturday Night* (Toronto: HarperCollins, 2014), 18.

12   Ibid., 203.

13   Ibid., 35.

14   Ibid., 36, 74, 388.

15   Ibid., 41.

16   Myra Bloom, "A Product of Its Time: A Review of Heather O'Neill's *The Girl
Who Was Saturday Night*," supplement, *Puritan* (Summer 2015), http://puritan

-magazine.com/a-product-of-its-time-a-review-of-heather-oneills-the-girl-who -was-saturday-night/. Bloom argues in part – I think convincingly – that the effect of O'Neill's novel is to set the Quebec nationalist movement as an artifact of another time, rather than as something with continued resonance in the present.

17 Gail Scott, *Main Brides* (Toronto: Coach House Books, 1993), 31, 130.

18 Gail Scott, *My Paris* (Toronto: Mercury, 1999).

19 O'Neill, *The Girl Who Was Saturday Night*, 328.

WHOSE MALLS? WALMART IN WHITEHORSE

1 William Leach, *Land of Desire: Merchants, Power, and the Rise of a New American Culture* (New York: Vintage, 1994).

2 The ongoing series of lawsuits began as Dukes v. Wal-Mart and was a suit seeking class action status at the Supreme Court level in the United States. It is now a series of state-by-state suits. See Brad Seligman, "Patriarchy at the Checkout Counter: The *Dukes v. Wal-Mart Stores, Inc.*, Class-Action Suit," *Wal-Mart: The Face of Twenty-First-Century Capitalism*, ed. Nelson Lichtenstein (New York and London: New Press, 2006), 231–42; as well as the *Wal-Mart Class Website*, walmartclass.com (n.d.).

3 Quite a few books have been published on Walmart from all positions across the political spectrum. A sampling of these works includes Nelson Lichtenstein, ed., *Wal-Mart: The Face of Twenty-First Century Capitalism* (New York and London: New Press, 2006); William H. Marquard with Bill Birchard, *Wal-Smart: What it Really Takes to Profit in a Wal-Mart World* (New York: McGraw-Hill, 2007); Charles Fishman, *The Wal-Mart Effect: How the World's Most Powerful Company Really Works – and How it's Transforming the American Economy* (New York: Penguin, 2006); Sandra S. Vance and Roy V. Scott, *Wal-Mart: A History of Sam Walton's Retail Phenomenon* (New York: Twayne Publishers, 1994); Hugo Meunier, *Wal-Mart: Journal d'un Associé* (Montréal: Lux Éditeur, 2015); Stanley D. Brunn, ed., *Wal-Mart World: The World's Biggest Corporation in the Global Economy* (New York and London: Routledge, 2006); Richard Vedder and Wendell Cox, *The Wal-Mart Revolution: How Big Box Stores Benefit Consumers, Workers, and the Economy* (Washington, DC: AEI Press, 2006); Bethany Moreton, *To Serve God and Wal-Mart* (Cambridge, MA, and London: Harvard University Press, 2009); and the film *Wal-Mart: The High Cost of Low Price*, dir. Robert Greenwald, 98 minutes, Brave New Films, 2005, which has an accompanying book: Greg Spotts, *Wal-Mart: The High Cost of Low Price* (New York: Disinformation, 2005).

4 Bethany Moreton has examined this issue in detail. She finds that "frequent Wal-Mart shopping correlates closely with conservative voting," and notes that a full eighty-five per cent of frequent Walmart shoppers voted for George W. Bush in the 2004 presidential election in *To Serve God and Wal-Mart*, 1.

5   *Mallrats*, prod. Caldecot Chubb, dir. Kevin Smith, 94 minutes, View Askew, 1995, DVD; *Dawn of the Dead*, prod. Richard P. Rubenstein, dir. George Romero, 156 minutes, Ultimate Final Cut, Laurel Group, 1978, DVD; *Where the Heart Is*, prod. Susan Cartsonis, dir. Matt Williams, 120 minutes, Twentieth Century Fox, 2000, DVD. *Where the Heart Is* is based on the novel of the same title by Billie Letts (New York: Warner Books, 1995).

6   Ken Cameron, *Dear Johnny Deere* (Edmonton: NeWest Press, 2015), 95.

7   Thomas King, *The Back of the Turtle* (Toronto: HarperCollins, 2014), 216.

8   Bethany Moreton's *To Serve God and Wal-Mart* provides a thorough, very good study of this correlation.

9   Robert Service, *The Cremation of Sam McGee* (Toronto: Kids Can Press, 1986); Robert Service, *The Shooting of Dan McGrew* (Toronto: Kids Can Press, 1986); (both were originally published in *Songs of a Sourdough*, 1907); Robert Kroetsch, *The Man From the Creeks* (Toronto: Random House, 1998).

10 See the note on Walmart's corporate website about RV parking, "Frequently Asked Questions," walmart.com (2016).

11 Pretty much every examination of Walmart notes that the company is the world's largest private employer. Charles Fishman, in *The Wal-Mart Effect*, suggests that not only is it the largest private employer, but that it "has become the most powerful, most influential company in the world" (5). *Forbes* lists Walmart as third, as I discuss, behind the US and Chinese militaries: Niall McCarthy, "The World's Biggest Employers," *Forbes*, 23 June 2015, https://www.forbes.com/sites/niallmccarthy/2015/06/23/the-worlds-biggest-employers-infographic/.

12 The impact of Walmart on different markets is a debated topic, but it seems that smaller stores do tend to shut down after Walmart arrives in town. I recommend David Karjanen, "The Wal-Mart Effect and the New Face of Capitalism: Labor Market and Community Impacts of the Megaretailer," in *Wal-Mart: The Face of Twenty-First-Century Capitalism*, ed. Lichtenstein, 143–62.

13 See Coyote's takedown of gender and pronouns in their collaborative book with Rae Spoon, *Gender Failure* (Vancouver: Arsenal Pulp Press, 2014).

14 Ivan E. Coyote, *The Slow Fix* (Vancouver: Arsenal Pulp Press, 2008), 132.

15 Ibid., 132.

16 Ibid., 132.

17 Ibid., 133.

18 Jeremy Rifkin, *The Age of Access: The New Culture of Hypercapitalism* (New York: TarcherPerigee, 2001).

19 Lisa Cooke, *North to Yukon: (Beyond) the Frontier in Canadian National-Cultural Imaginaries* (doctoral dissertation; Toronto: York University, 2009), 113.

20 By 2006, Charles Fishman, in *The Wal-Mart Effect*, was able to state that "more than half of all Americans live within five miles of a Wal-Mart store" and that "ninety percent of Americans live within fifteen miles of a Wal-Mart" (5).

21 Statistics Canada notes that northern climates "have seen some of the largest increases in temperatures over the past 60 years," "Section 1: Climate change in Canada," *Statistics Canada*, 27 November 2015, http://www.statcan.gc.ca/pub /16-201-x/2007000/10542-eng.htm.

22 Coyote, *The Slow Fix*, 145.

23 Ibid., 148.

CRACKS IN THE CONCRETE: KITSILANO AND BEYOND

1   About sixty-five per cent of Kitsilano dwellers were renters in the 2001 census. See Canada Mortgage and Housing Corporation, "Comparing Neighbourhoods – Vancouver," *Canada Mortgage and Housing Corporation*, 2016, https:// www.cmhc-schl.gc.ca/en/co/buho/sune/sune_007.cfm.

2   There is a longer history connected to waterfronts in Vancouver becoming associated with the middle and wealthy classes; at one point, waterfronts were largely industrial, working spaces or else impoverished, less desirable spaces. Before that, they were natural spaces that supported a wide mix of flora and fauna. In a literary context, one might think of Malcolm Lowry's shack in Dollarton, now part of North Vancouver. False Creek, the site of Granville Island, is a former industrial location that has been subject to multiple waves of planned gentrification. See, for instance, the City of Vancouver, "Southeast False Creek," vancouver.ca, 2016, http://vancouver.ca/home-property-development /southeast-false-creek.aspx. See also Catherine Gourley, *Island in the Creek: The Granville Island Story* (Madeira Park, BC: Harbour, 1988).

3   Roy Miki, *Mannequin Rising* (Vancouver: Talonbooks, 2011), 53.

4   Alisa Smith and J.B. MacKinnon, *The 100-Mile Diet: A Year of Local Eating* (Toronto: Random House, 2007).

5   Miki, *Mannequin Rising*, 54.

6   Ibid., 57.

7   Ibid., 62.

8   There is a huge amount to say about the Downtown Eastside. Much of it, however, does not feel like it is mine to say, as I am not part of that contested community. One place to start looking is Brad Cran and Gillian Jerome's *Hope in Shadows: Stories and Photographs of Vancouver's Downtown Eastside* (Vancouver: Arsenal Pulp Press, 2008). It is a challenging space to write about for many reasons and, in general, is best documented by residents of the community itself. There are many non-fiction accounts, but on the cultural and literary side, books like Bud Osborn's *Hundred Block Rock* (Vancouver: Arsenal Pulp Press, 1999) and Eden Robinson's *Blood Sports* (Toronto: McClelland & Stewart, 2007) perhaps provide useful starting points.

9   Miki, *Mannequin Rising*, 14.

10 This and the previous two quotations from Miki, *Mannequin Rising*, 13–14.

11 See Louise Story, "'Seaweed' Clothing Has None, Tests Show," *New York Times*, 14 November 2007, http://www.nytimes.com/2007/11/14/business/14seaweed .html.

12 Miki, *Mannequin Rising*, 30–31.

13 See, for instance, the influential, if older, study of how urban practices like city walking and dioramas lead to elements of modern cinematic practices in Anne Friedberg's *Window Shopping: Cinema and the Postmodern* (Oakland: University of California Press, 1994).

14 See Andrew Turgeon, "The Great Pacific Garbage Patch," *National Geographic*, 19 September 2014, https://www.nationalgeographic.org/encyclopedia/great -pacific-garbage-patch/.

15 Lisa Robertson, *Occasional Work and Seven Walks from the Office of Soft Architecture*, 3rd ed. (Toronto: Coach House Books, 2011).

16 Timothy Taylor, *Stanley Park* (Toronto: Vintage, 2001).

17 Michael Kluckner, *Vanishing Vancouver: The Last 25 Years* (Vancouver: Whitecap, 2012); Douglas Coupland, *City of Glass*, revised edition (Vancouver: Douglas & McIntyre, 2009). See Coupland's note on Kitsilano on page 82 in particular.

18 A brief recommendation on poetry concerned with waterways, including Vancouver's: Rita Wong's *Undercurrent* (Gibsons, BC: Nightwood, 2015).

19 Michael Turner, *Kingsway* (Vancouver: Arsenal Pulp Press, 1995), 9.

20 Ibid., 43.

21 Elaine Chau, "Richmond Chinese-language only sign controversy, a sign of cultural tension," *CBC News*, 12 March 2015, http://www.cbc.ca/news/canada /british-columbia/richmond-chinese-language-only-sign-controversy-a-sign -of-cultural-tension-1.2991836.

22 Turner, *Kingsway*, 63–64.

23 Douglas Coupland, *The Gum Thief* (Toronto: Vintage, 2007).

24 Miki, *Mannequin Rising*, 75.

BIGGER IS BIGGER: WEST EDMONTON MALL

1 Tristin Hopper, "Canada's Strip Malls Crumble toward Extinction," *National Post*, 13 November 2011, http://nationalpost.com/news/canada/canadas -strip-malls-crumbles-toward-extinction/wcm/4191b00b-f5e9-4385-89c0 -2deb90bccc9b.

2 Rem Koolhaas, Chuihua Judy Chung, Jeffrey Inaba and Sze Tsung Leong, eds., *The Harvard Design School Guide to Shopping* (Los Angeles: Taschen, 2001). Fredric Jameson reflects upon this book in his essay "Future City," *New Left Review* 21 (2003), 65–79.

3 All of the quotations from the poems come from Heather Spears, *The Word for Sand* (Toronto: Wolsak and Wynn, 1988), 75–82.

4   Tom van Riper, "The World's Largest Malls," *Forbes.com*, 18 January 2008, https://www.forbes.com/2008/01/17/retail-malls-shopping-biz-commerce-cx_tvr_0118malls.html. There are various online sources for this ranking; at the moment, the South China Mall seems to win all measures for size.

5   Mark MacKinnon, "China's Giant, Deserted Malls Wait for Reluctant Customers," *Globe and Mail*, 2 October 2011, https://www.theglobeandmail.com/news/world/chinas-giant-deserted-malls-wait-for-reluctant-consumers/article555588/.

6   The mall was "relaunched" in 2015 and seems to be busier now: Johan Nylander, "Chinese 'ghost mall' back from the dead?" *CNN.com*, 24 June 2015, http://www.cnn.com/2015/04/28/asia/china-ghost-mall-return-to-life/index.html.

7   Walter Benjamin, *The Arcades Project*, trans. Howard Eiland and Kevin McLaughlin (Cambridge, MA: Harvard University Press, 1999), 13.

8   Slavoj Žižek, *Living in the End Times* (London: Verso, 2010), 263.

9   Lisa Robertson, *Occasional Work and Seven Walks from the Office of Soft Architecture*, 3rd ed. (Toronto: Coach House Books, 2011), 182.

10 Jeff Derksen, "Compression," *Transnational Muscle Cars* (Vancouver: Talonbooks, 2010), 106.

11 Žižek, *Living in the End Times*, 255.

12 M. Jeffrey Hardwick, *Mall Maker: Victor Gruen, Architect of an American Dream* (Philadelphia: University of Pennsylvania Press, 2003), 144.

13 Victor Gruen, *The Heart of Our Cities: The Urban Crisis: Diagnosis and Cure* (New York: Simon & Schuster, 1964), 53.

14 Just a couple of examples: Geoffrey Baker and Bruno Funaro, *Shopping Centers: Design and Operation* (New York: Reinhold, 1951); and Donald L. Curtiss, *Operation Shopping Centers: Guidebook to Effective Management & Promotion* (Washington, DC: Urban Land Institute, 1961).

15 Hardwick, in *Mall Maker*, writes, "it was hardly a secret that the suburban experience, and especially the shopping center, was premised on creating a separate, private space for whites" (152). Gruen's own writing is also helpful, such as the book by him and Larry Smith, *Shopping Towns USA* (New York: Reinhold, 1960), or Gruen's *The Heart of Our Cities*.

16 See Joseph Heath and Andrew Potter, *The Rebel Sell: Why the Culture Can't Be Jammed* (Toronto: HarperCollins, 2004). While I disagree with some of their conclusions, the book is a useful critique.

17 Jeff Derksen, "'Closer to a Work of Art than a Simple Material Product': A Material Poetics of the Urban," Material Cultures: The Canadian Literature Symposium, University of Ottawa, 8 May 2011.

18 Hardwick, *Mall Maker*, 2.

19 See Gareth Hampshire, "Indigenous Edmontonian alleges racial profiling after being ejected from Kingsway Mall," *CBC News*, 15 April 2016, http://www

.cbc.ca/news/canada/edmonton/indigenous-edmontonian-alleges-profiling
-after-being-ejected-from-kingsway-mall-1.3536100; Gareth Hampshire and
Scott Lilwall, "Aboriginal outreach worker Gary Moostoos banned from City
Centre Mall," *CBC News*, 28 October 2014, http://www.cbc.ca/news/canada
/edmonton/aboriginal-outreach-worker-gary-moostoos-banned-from-city
-centre-mall-1.2816394.

20 See especially Margaret MacKeith, *The History and Conservation of Shopping
Arcades* (London and New York: Mansell, 1986); and Johann Friedrich Geist,
Arcades: The History of a Building Type, trans. Jane O. Newman and John H.
Smith (1979; Cambridge, MA: MIT Press, 1983).

21 Jane Jacobs, *The Death and Life of Great American Cities* (New York: Vintage,
1961), 4.

22 Jacobs, *Death and Life*, 162.

23 "3 Hurled to Death in Canada as Roller Coaster Derails in Mall," *Los Angeles
Times*, 16 June 1986, http://articles.latimes.com/1986-06-16/news/mn-10861
_1_roller-coaster-derails.

24 "The last Edmonton dolphin, Howard, dies," *CBC News*, 7 May 2005, http://
www.cbc.ca/news/canada/the-last-edmonton-dolphin-howard-dies-1.531747.

25 Daniel Herman, "Mall: Requiem for a Type," *The Harvard Design School Guide
to Shopping: Harvard Design School Project on the City*, eds. Rem Koolhaas, Chuihua Judy Chung, Jeffrey Inaba and Sze Tsung Leong (Los Angeles: Taschen,
2001), 466.

26 The site is abandonedtargetsofcanada.tumblr.com. The dismal failure of
the US discount store Target to find customers in Canada marks a surprising recent event in the Canadian retail landscape that should remind us that
Canada and the US are quite distinct markets. For a quick take on the issue,
see Tamsin McMahon, "Missing the mark: Five reasons why Target failed in
Canada," *Globe and Mail*, 15 January 2015, https://www.theglobeandmail.com
/report-on-business/missing-the-mark-5-reasons-why-target-failed-in-canad/
article22459819/.

27 Benjamin, *The Arcades Project*, 112.

28 Janice Williamson, "Notes on Storyville North: Circulating West Edmonton
Mall," *LifeStyle Shopping: The Subject of Consumption*, ed. Rob Shields (London:
Routledge, 1992), 216–32.

29 Vivek Shraya, ed., *The Magnificent Malls of Edmonton*, 2015, https://vivekshraya
.com/books/the-magnificent-malls-of-edmonton/.

CONCLUSION: RETAIL THERAPY

1 Todd Babiak, *The Garneau Block* (Toronto: McClelland & Stewart, 2006), 211.

2 See Lily Cho, *Eating Chinese: Culture on the Menu in Small Town Canada* (Toronto:
University of Toronto Press, 2010).

3   *Fubar*, prod. and dir. Michael Dowse, 76 minutes, Busted Tranny, 2002, DVD; *Fubar 2: Balls to the Wall*, prod. and dir. Michael Dowse, 85 minutes, FU2 Productions, 2010, DVD.

4   A recent US study finds that twenty-three per cent of mobile phone users occasionally use their phones in order to avoid interacting with others when in public spaces. See Lee Rainie and Kathryn Zickuhr, "Americans' Views on Mobile Etiquette," *Pew Research Centre*, 26 August 2015, http://www.pewinternet.org/2015/08/26/americans-views-on-mobile-etiquette/.

5   *waydowntown*, prod. Gary Burns and Shirley Vercruysse, dir. Gary Burns, 87 minutes, Burns Film Ltd., 2000, DVD.

6   CBC News, "Suicide rate in Alberta climbs 30% in wake of mass oilpatch layoffs," *CBC News*, 7 December 2015, http://www.cbc.ca/news/canada/calgary/suicide-rate-alberta-increase-layoffs-1.3353662.

7   George Melnyk, "It's a Job and You Have to Do It Every Day: Gary Burns," *The Young, the Restless, and the Dead: Interviews with Canadian Filmmakers*, vol. 1, ed. George Melnyk (Waterloo: Wilfrid Laurier University Press, 2008), 88.

8   See Katherine Monk, *Weird Sex & Snowshoes: And Other Canadian Film Phenomena* (Vancouver: Raincoast, 2001).

9   On Idle No More, see Ken Coates, *#IdleNoMore: And the Remaking of Canada* (Regina: University of Regina Press, 2015); and especially the Kino-nda-niimi Collective, *The Winter We Danced: Voices from the Past, the Future, and the Idle No More Movement* (Winnipeg: Arbeiter Ring, 2014).

10 Wab Kinew, *The Reason You Walk* (Toronto: Viking, 2015), 226.

11 Amanda Holpuch, "Black Lives Matter Protest Shuts Down Mall of America and Airport Terminal," *Guardian*, 23 December 2015, https://www.theguardian.com/us-news/2015/dec/23/black-lives-matter-organizers-protest-mall-of-america.

12 See Michel de Certeau, *The Practice of Everyday Life*, trans. Steven F. Rendall (Berkeley: University of California Press, 1984).

Works Cited

Abandoned Targets of Canada. Last modified November 22, 2015. Accessed April 23, 2016. https://abandonedtargetsofcanada.tumblr.com/archive.

Babiak, Todd. *The Garneau Block*. Toronto: McClelland & Stewart, 2006.

Baker, Geoffrey, and Bruno Funaro. *Shopping Centers: Design and Operation*. New York: Reinhold, 1951.

Batten, Jack. *Honest Ed's Story: The Crazy Rags to Riches Story of Ed Mirvish*. Toronto: Doubleday Canada, 1972.

Bauman, Zygmunt. *Consuming Life*. Cambridge: Polity Press, 2007.

Belisle, Donica. *Retail Nation: Department Stores and the Making of Modern Canada*. Vancouver: UBC Press, 2011.

Benjamin, Walter. *The Arcades Project*. Trans. Howard Eiland and Kevin McLaughlin. Cambridge: Harvard University Press, 1999.

Bloom, Myra. "A Product of Its Time: A Review of Heather O'Neill's 'The Girl Who Was Saturday Night.'" In supplement, *Puritan* (Summer 2015). Accessed June 15 2016. http://puritan-magazine.com/a-product-of-its-time-a-review-of-heather-oneills-the-girl-who-was-saturday-night/.

Brunn, Stanley D., ed. *Wal-Mart World: The World's Biggest Corporation in the Global Economy*. New York, London: Routledge, 2006.

"Calgary downtown vacancy rate moving toward 25%." *CBC News*. June 1, 2016. Accessed on June 5, 2017. http://www.cbc.ca/news/canada/calgary/office-space-vacancy-rising-1.3611785.

Cameron, Ken. *Dear Johnny Deere*. Edmonton: NeWest Press, 2015.

Canada Mortgage and Housing Corporation. "Comparing Neighbour-hoods – Vancouver." Accessed April 25, 2016. https://www.cmhc-schl.gc.ca/en/co/buho/sune/sune_007.cfm.

Carrier, Roch. *The Hockey Sweater*. Trans. Sheila Fischman. Toronto: Tundra Books, 1984.

Chan, Weyman. *Chinese Blue*. Vancouver: Talonbooks, 2012.

Chau, Elaine. "Richmond Chinese-language only sign controversy, a sign of cultural tension." *CBC News*. March 12, 2015. Accessed June 16, 2016. http://www.cbc.ca/news/canada/british-columbia/richmond-chinese-language-only-sign-controversy-a-sign-of-cultural-tension-1.2991836.

Cho, Lily. *Eating Chinese: Culture on the Menu in Small Town Canada*. Toronto: University of Toronto Press, 2011.

The City of Vancouver. "Southeast False Creek." *Vancouver.ca*. Accessed April 25, 2016. http://vancouver.ca/home-property-development/southeast-false-creek.aspx.

Coates, Ken. *#IdleNoMore: And the Remaking of Canada*. Regina: University of Regina Press, 2015.

Cooke, Lisa. *North to Yukon: (Beyond) the Frontier in Canadian National-Cultural Imaginaries*. PhD diss., York University, 2009.

Coupland, Douglas. *City of Glass*. Rev. ed. Vancouver: Douglas & Mc-Intyre, 2009.

———. *The Gum Thief*. Toronto: Vintage, 2007.

Coyote, Ivan E. *The Slow Fix*. Vancouver: Arsenal Pulp Press, 2008.

Coyote, Ivan E., and Rae Spoon. *Gender Failure*. Vancouver: Arsenal Pulp Press, 2014.

Cran, Brad, and Gillian Jerome. *Hope in Shadows: Stories and Photographs of Vancouver's Downtown Eastside*. Vancouver: Arsenal Pulp Press, 2008.

CrossIron Mills. "CrossIron Mills Story." Accessed April 23, 2016. https://www.crossironmills.com/about-us/about-crossiron-mills/.

"A Crowd Larger than Red Deer Hits up Calgary's Chinook Mall for Boxing Day." *660 News*. December 27, 2014. Accessed January 7, 2015. http://www.660news.com/2014/12/27/a-crowd-larger-than -red-deer-hits-up-calgarys-chinook-mall-for-boxing-day/.

Curtiss, Donald L. *Operation Shopping Centers: Guidebook to Effective Management & Promotion*. Washington, DC: Urban Land Institute, 1961.

D'Aliesio, Renata. "Tapped Out: Water Woes, Part One." *Calgary Herald*. November 30, 2007. Accessed April 23, 2016. http://www .calgaryherald.com/tapped+water+woes+part/906447/story.html.

Dawn of the Dead. Directed by George Romero. 1978. Ultimate Final Cut. Laurel Group, Inc. DVD.

De Certeau, Michel. *The Practice of Everyday Life*. Trans. Steven F. Rendall. Berkeley: University of California Press, 1984.

Derksen, Jeff. "'Closer to a Work of Art than a Simple Material Product': A Material Poetics of the Urban." *Material Cultures: The Canadian Literature Symposium*. University of Ottawa, May 8, 2011.

———. *Transnational Muscle Cars*. Vancouver: Talonbooks, 2003.

Eagleton, Terry. *Ideology: An Introduction*. London: Verso, 1991.

Easterbrook, W.T., and Hugh G.J. Aitken. *Canadian Economic History*. Toronto: Macmillan, 1956.

Fishman, Charles. *The Wal-Mart Effect*. New York: Penguin Books, 2006.

Fiske, John. "Shopping for Pleasure: Malls, Power, and Resistance." In *The Consumer Society Reader*, edited by Juliet B. Schor and Douglas B. Holt, 306–28. New York: New Press, 2000.

Freure, Jason. "A 19-Year-Old's Referendum: An Interview with Heather O'Neill." In supplement, *Puritan* (Summer 2015). Accessed June 15, 2016. http://puritan-magazine.com/a-19-year-olds-referendum -an-interview-with-heather-oneill/.

Friedberg, Anne. *Window Shopping: Cinema and the Postmodern*. Oakland: University of California Press, 1994.

Fubar. Directed by Michael Dowse. 2002. Busted Tranny. DVD.

Fubar 2: Balls to the Wall. Directed by Michael Dowse. 2010. FU2 Productions. DVD.

Geist, Johann Friedrich. *Arcades: The History of a Building Type.* Translated by Jane O. Newman and John H. Smith. Cambridge, MA: MIT Press, 1983.

Germain, Jean-Claude. *Of Jesuits and Bohemians.* Translated by Donald Winkler. Montreal: Véhicule Press, 2015.

Glancey, Jonathan. "The Death of the US Shopping Mall." *BBC Culture.* October 21, 2014. Accessed January 7, 2015. http://www.bbc.com /culture/story/20140411-is-the-shopping-mall-dead.

Gourley, Catherine. *Island in the Creek: The Granville Island Story.* Madeira Park, BC: Harbour, 1988.

Gruen, Victor. *The Heart of Our Cities: The Urban Crisis: Diagnosis and Cure.* New York: Simon & Schuster, 1964.

Gruen, Victor, and Larry Smith. *Shopping Town USA: The Planning of Shopping Centers.* New York: Reinhold, 1960.

Halberstam, Judith. *Queer Art of Failure.* Durham: Duke University Press, 2011.

Hall, David. *A True Urban Centre: Collaborative Community Problem-Solving and the Dufferin Mall.* Toronto: Caledon Institute for Social Policy, 1997.

Hampshire, Gareth. "Indigenous Edmontonian alleges racial profiling after being ejected from Kingsway Mall." *CBC News.* April 15, 2016. Accessed June 15, 2016. http://www.cbc.ca/news/canada /edmonton/indigenous-edmontonian-alleges-profiling-after-being -ejected-from-kingsway-mall-1.3536100.

Hampshire, Gareth, and Scott Lilwall. "Aboriginal outreach worker Gary Moostoos banned from City Centre Mall." *CBC News.* October 28, 2014. Accessed June 15, 2016. http://www.cbc.ca/news/canada /edmonton/aboriginal-outreach-worker-gary-moostoos-banned -from-city-centre-mall-1.2816394.

Hardwick, M. Jeffrey. *Mall Maker: Victor Gruen, Architect of an American Dream.* Philadelphia: University of Pennsylvania Press, 2004.

Herman, Daniel. "Mall: Requiem for a Type." In *The Harvard Design School Guide to Shopping,* edited by Rem Koolhaas, Sze Tsung Leong, Chuihua Judy Chung and Jeffrey Inaba. Los Angeles: Taschen, 2001.

Holpuch, Amanda. "Black Lives Matter Protest Shuts Down Mall of America and Airport Terminal." *Guardian*. December 25, 2015. Accessed April 25, 2016. https://www.theguardian.com/us-news/2015/dec/23/black-lives-matter-organizers-protest-mall-of-america.

Hopper, Tristin. "Canada's Strip Malls Crumble toward Extinction." *National Post*. November 13, 2011. Accessed January 7, 2015. http://nationalpost.com/news/canada/canadas-strip-malls-crumbles-toward-extinction/wcm/4191b00b-f5e9-4385-89c0-2deb90bccc9b.

Horbulyk, Theodore. "Liquid Gold? Water Markets in Canada." *Eau Canada: The Future of Canada's Water*, edited by Karen Bakker, 205–18. Vancouver: UBC Press, 2007.

Hutcheon, Linda. *Splitting Images: Contemporary Canadian Ironies*. Toronto: Oxford University Press Canada, 1991.

Innis, Harold. *The Fur Trade in Canada*. 1930. Toronto: University of Toronto Press, 1977.

Iyer, Pico. *The Global Soul: Jet Lag, Shopping Malls, and the Search for Home*. London: Bloomsbury, 2000.

Jacobs, Jane. *The Death and Life of Great American Cities*. New York: Random House, 1961.

"Justin Bieber Takes Selfie with Fashion Santa at Yorkdale." *CBC News*. December 19, 2015. Accessed April 25, 2016. http://www.cbc.ca/news/canada/toronto/bieber-selfie-fashion-selfie-1.3373624.

Karjanen, David. "The Wal-Mart Effect and the New Face of Capitalism: Labor Market and Community Impacts of the Megaretailer." In *Wal-Mart: The Face of Twenty-First Century Capitalism*, edited by Nelson Lichtenstein, 143–62. New York and London: New Press, 2006.

Kinew, Wab. *The Reason You Walk*. Toronto: Viking, 2015.

King, Thomas. *The Back of the Turtle*. Toronto: HarperCollins, 2014.

———. *Green Grass, Running Water*. Toronto: HarperCollins, 1993.

Kino-nda-niimi Collective. *The Winter We Danced: Voices from the Past, the Future, and the Idle No More Movement*. Winnipeg: Arbeiter Ring, 2014.

Klein, Naomi. *This Changes Everything: Capitalism vs. the Climate.* Toronto: Knopf, 2014.

Kluckner, Michael. *Vanishing Vancouver: The Last 25 Years.* Vancouver: Whitecap Books, 2012.

Koolhaas, Rem, Sze Tsung Leong, Chuihua Judy Chung, and Jeffrey Inaba, editors. *Harvard Design School Guide to Shopping: Harvard Design School Project on the City.* Los Angeles: Taschen, 2001.

Kopytek, Bruce Allen. *Eaton's: The Trans-Canada Store.* Charleston: History Press, 2014.

Kroetsch, Robert. *Alberta.* 2nd ed. Edmonton: NeWest Press, 1993.

———. *The Man From the Creeks.* Toronto: Random House, 1998.

"The last Edmonton dolphin, Howard, dies." *CBC News.* May 7, 2005. Accessed June 15, 2016. http://www.cbc.ca/news/canada/the-last -edmonton-dolphin-howard-dies-1.531747.

Leach, William. *Land of Desire: Merchants, Power, and the Rise of a New American Culture.* New York: Vintage, 1994.

Lebhar, Godfrey M. *The Chain Store – Boon or Bane?* New York: Harper & Brothers, 1932.

Letts, Billie. *Where the Heart Is.* New York: Warner Books, 1995.

"Life Sentence for Jane Creba Murder." *CBC News.* December 22, 2009. Accessed April 25, 2016. http://www.cbc.ca/news/canada/toronto /life-sentence-for-jane-creba-murder-1.845433.

The Living Water Project. "Alberta Water Policy Data." Accessed April 23, 2016. http://www.waterpolicy.ca/alberta-water-policy.

Lousley, Cheryl. "'Hosanna Da, Our Home on Natives' Land': Environmental Justice and Democracy in Thomas King's 'Green Grass, Running Water.'" *Essays on Canadian Writing* 81, no.1 (2004): 17–44.

MacKeith, Margaret. *The History and Conservation of Shopping Arcades.* London and New York: Mansell, 1986.

MacKinnon, Mark. "China's Giant, Deserted Malls Wait for Reluctant Customers." *Globe and Mail.* October 22, 2011. Accessed January 7, 2015. https://www.theglobeandmail.com/news/world/chinas -giant-deserted-malls-wait-for-reluctant-consumers/article555588/.

Mallrats. Directed by Kevin Smith. 1995. View Askew. DVD.

Marquard, William H. *Wal-Smart: What it Really Takes to Profit in a Wal-Mart World.* New York: McGraw-Hill, 2007.

McCarthy, Niall. "The World's Biggest Employers." *Forbes.* June 23, 2015. Accessed June 15, 2016. https://www.forbes.com/sites/niallmccarthy/2015/06/23/the-worlds-biggest-employers-infographic/#4ff03428686b.

McMahon, Tamsin. "Missing the Mark: Five Reasons Why Target Failed in Canada." *Globe and Mail.* January 15, 2015. Accessed April 23, 2016. https://www.theglobeandmail.com/report-on-business/missing-the-mark-5-reasons-why-target-failed-in-canad/article22459819/.

Melnyk, George. *Film and the City: The Urban Imaginary in Canadian Cinema.* Edmonton: Athabasca University Press, 2014.

———, editor. *The Young, the Restless, and the Dead: Interviews with Canadian Filmmakers.* Vol. 1. Waterloo: Wilfrid Laurier University Press, 2008.

Meunier, Hugo. *Wal-Mart: Journal d'un Associé.* Montreal: Lux Éditeur, 2015.

Miki, Roy. *Mannequin Rising.* Vancouver: New Star Books, 2011.

Monet, Claude. *La grande allée à Giverny,* 1900. Oil on Canvas. Montreal Museum of Fine Arts.

Monk, Katherine. *Weird Sex & Snowshoes: And Other Canadian Film Phenomena.* Vancouver: Raincoast, 2001.

Moreton, Bethany. *To Serve God and Wal-Mart.* Cambridge, London: Harvard University Press, 2009.

Nylander, Johan. "Chinese 'ghost mall' back from the dead?" *CNN.com.* June 24, 2015. Accessed June 15, 2016. http://www.cnn.com/2015/04/28/asia/china-ghost-mall-return-to-life/index.html.

O'Malley, Bryan Lee. *Scott Pilgrim & The Infinite Sadness.* Portland: Oni Press, 2006.

———. *Scott Pilgrim Gets It Together.* Portland: Oni Press, 2007.

O'Neill, Heather. *The Girl Who Was Saturday Night.* Toronto: HarperCollins, 2014.

———. *Lullabies for Little Criminals*. New York: Harper Perennial, 2006.

Osborn, Bud. *Hundred Block Rock*. Vancouver: Arsenal Pulp Press, 1999.

Perkel, Colin. "Man Admits Shooting Up Eaton Centre Food Court, Says It Wasn't Planned." *Globe and Mail*. October 10, 2014. Accessed April 25, 2016. https://www.theglobeandmail.com/news/toronto/man-admits-shooting-up-eaton-centre-mall-food-court-but-says-it-wasnt-planned/article21063246/.

Peterson, Hayley. "America's Shopping Malls Are Dying a Slow, Ugly Death." *Business Insider*. January 31, 2014. Accessed January 7, 2015. http://www.businessinsider.com/shopping-malls-are-going-extinct-2014-1.

Potter, Andrew, and Joseph Heath. *The Rebel Sell: Why the Culture Can't Be Jammed*. Toronto: Harper Perennial, 2005.

Rainie, Lee, and Kathryn Zickuhr. "Americans' Views on Mobile Etiquette." *Pew Research Centre*. August 26, 2015. Accessed June 16, 2016. http://www.pewinternet.org/2015/08/26/americans-views-on-mobile-etiquette/.

Rhodes, Richard. "Michael Snow: The Public Commissions." In *The Michael Snow Project: Visual Art, 1951–1993*, edited by Dennis Reid, Philip Monk, Louise Dompierre, Richard Rhodes and Derrick de Kerckhove, 478–97. Toronto: Art Gallery of Ontario, The Power Plant and Knopf Canada, 1994.

Richler, Mordecai. *Son of a Smaller Hero*. 1955. Toronto: McClelland & Stewart, 2002.

———. *The Street*. Toronto: Penguin Books, 1985.

Rifkin, Jeremy. *The Age of Access: The New Culture of Hypercapitalism*. New York: Tarcher, 2001.

Robertson, Lisa. *Occasional Work and Seven Walks from the Office of Soft Architecture*. 3rd ed. Toronto: Coach House Books, 2011.

Robinson, Eden. *Blood Sports*. Toronto: McClelland & Stewart, 2007.

Ross, Sinclair. *As For Me and My House*. 1941. Toronto: McClelland & Stewart, 2008.

Rushkoff, Douglas. *Coercion: Why We Listen to What "They" Say*. New York: Riverhead, 1999.

Schindler, David. "Forward." In *Eau Canada: The Future of Canada's Water*, edited by Karen Bakker, xiii–xiv. Vancouver: UBC Press, 2007.

Schwartz, Nelson D. "The Economics (and Nostalgia) of Dead Malls." *New York Times*. January 5, 2015. Accessed January 5, 2015. https://www.nytimes.com/2015/01/04/business/the-economics-and-nostalgia-of-dead-malls.html.

Scott, Gail. *Main Brides*. Toronto: Coach House Books, 1993.

———. *My Paris*. Toronto: Mercury Press, 1999.

Seligman, Brad. "Patriarchy at the Checkout Counter: The Dukes v. Wal-Mart Stores, Inc., Class-Action Suit." In *Wal-Mart: The Face of Twenty-First Century Capitalism*, edited by Nelson Lichtenstein, 231–42. New York and London: New Press, 2006.

Service, Robert. *The Cremation of Sam McGee*. Toronto: Kids Can Press, 1986.

———. *The Shooting of Dan McGrew*. Toronto: Kids Can Press, 1986.

Shraya, Vivek. "If These Malls Could Talk." *vivekshraya.com*. May 15, 2015. Accessed June 5, 2017. https://vivekshraya.com/essays/if-these-malls-could-talk/.

Smith, Alisa, and J.B. MacKinnon. *The 100-Mile Diet: A Year of Local Eating*. Toronto: Random House, 2007.

Snow v. Eaton Centre (1982) 70 CPR (2d) 105, OJ No 3645.

Spears, Heather. *The Word for Sand*. Hamilton: Wolsak and Wynn, 1988.

Spotts, Greg. *Wal-Mart: The High Cost of Low Price*. New York: Disinformation, 2005.

Sprague, John. "Great Wet North? Canada's Myth of Water Abundance." In *Eau Canada: The Future of Canada's Water*, edited by Karen Bakker, 29–30. Vancouver: UBC Press, 2007.

Statistics Canada. "Section 1: Climate change in Canada." November 27, 2015. Accessed June 15, 2016. http://www.statcan.gc.ca/pub/16-201-x/2007000/10542-eng.htm.

Stoekl, Allan. *Bataille's Peak: Energy, Religion, Postsustainability*. Minneapolis: University of Minnesota Press, 2007.

Story, Louise. "'Seaweed' Clothing Has None, Tests Show." *New York Times*. November 14, 2007. Accessed April 25, 2016. http://www.nytimes.com/2007/11/14/business/14seaweed.html.

"Suicide Rate in Alberta Climbs 30% in Wake of Mass Oilpatch Layoffs." *CBC News*. December 7, 2015. Accessed April 25, 2016. http://www.cbc.ca/news/canada/calgary/suicide-rate-alberta-increase-layoffs-1.3353662.

The Sweater. Directed by Sheldon Cohen. 1980. National Film Board. Accessed August 21, 2017. https://www.nfb.ca/film/sweater/.

Taylor, Timothy. *Stanley Park*. Toronto: Vintage, 2001.

"3 Hurled to Death in Canada as Roller Coaster Derails in Mall." *Los Angeles Times*. June 16, 1986. Accessed January 7, 2016. http://articles.latimes.com/1986-06-16/news/mn-10861_1_roller-coaster-derails.

Turgeon, Andrew. "The Great Pacific Garbage Patch." *National Geographic*. September 19, 2014. Accessed June 16, 2016. https://www.nationalgeographic.org/encyclopedia/great-pacific-garbage-patch/.

Turner, Michael. *Kingsway*. Vancouver: Arsenal Pulp Press, 1995.

Uberti, David. "The Death of the American Mall." *Guardian*. June 19, 2014. Accessed January 7 2015. https://www.theguardian.com/cities/2014/jun/19/-sp-death-of-the-american-shopping-mall.

Vance, Sandra S., and Roy V. Scott. *Wal-Mart: A History of Sam Walton's Retail Phenomenon*. New York: Twayne, 2015.

Van Herk, Aritha. *Mavericks: An Incorrigible History of Alberta*. Toronto: Penguin, 2001.

Van Riper, Tom. "The World's Largest Malls." *Forbes*. January 18, 2008. Accessed January 7, 2015. https://www.forbes.com/2008/01/17/retail-malls-shopping-biz-commerce-cx_tvr_0118malls.html.

Vassanji, M.G. *Mordecai Richler*. Toronto: Penguin, 2009.

Vedder, Richard, and Wendell Cox. *The Wal-Mart Revolution*. Washington, DC: AEI Press, 2006.

Wal-Mart: The High Cost of Low Price. Directed by Robert Greenwald. 2005. Brave New Films. DVD.

Walmart. "Frequently Asked Questions." Accessed April 25, 2016. http://corporate.walmart.com/frequently-asked-questions.

Watkins, Mel H. "A Staple Theory of Economic Growth." 1963. In *Staples and Beyond: Selected Writings of Mel Watkins,* edited by Hugh Grant and David A. Wolfe, 5–29. Montreal and Kingston: McGill-Queen's University Press, 2006.

Wattles, Jackie. "Stores are closing at an epic pace." *CNN Money.* April 22, 2017. Accessed June 5, 2017. http://money.cnn.com/2017/04/22/news/credit-suisse-retail/index.html.

Where the Heart Is. Directed by Matt Williams. 2000. Twentieth Century Fox. DVD.

Williamson, Janice. "Notes on Storyville North: Circling West Edmonton Mall." In *LifeStyle Shopping: The Subject of Consumption,* edited by Rob Shields, 216–32. London: Routledge, 1992.

Wong, Rita. *Undercurrent.* Gibsons, BC: Nightwood, 2015.

World Wildlife Fund. "Canada's Rivers at Risk: Environmental Flows and Canada's Freshwater Future." Accessed April 23, 2016. http://assets.wwf.ca/downloads/canadas_rivers_at_risk.pdf.

Žižek, Slavoj. *Living in the End Times.* London: Verso, 2010.

———. *Mapping Ideology.* London: Verso, 1995.

Zola, Émile. *The Ladies' Paradise.* Translated by Brian Nelson. Oxford: Oxford University Press, 1995.

Kit Dobson works and writes in Calgary. He has lived across Canada and in the UK. The author or editor of three academic books, he is also the editor of *Please, No More Poetry: The Poetry of derek beaulieu* and a faculty member at Mount Royal University.